Thomas Edward Scrutton

Land in Fetters

The History and Policy of the Laws Restraining the Alienation and Settlement of

Land in England

Thomas Edward Scrutton

Land in Fetters
The History and Policy of the Laws Restraining the Alienation and Settlement of Land in England

ISBN/EAN: 9783744692946

Printed in Europe, USA, Canada, Australia, Japan

Cover: Foto ©ninafisch / pixelio.de

More available books at **www.hansebooks.com**

LAND IN FETTERS

London: C. J. CLAY AND SONS,
CAMBRIDGE UNIVERSITY PRESS WAREHOUSE,
AVE MARIA LANE.

Cambridge: DEIGHTON, BELL AND CO.
Leipzig: F. A. BROCKHAUS.

LAND IN FETTERS

OR

THE HISTORY AND POLICY OF THE LAWS RESTRAINING
THE ALIENATION AND SETTLEMENT OF LAND
IN ENGLAND.

BEING THE YORKE PRIZE ESSAY OF THE UNIVERSITY
OF CAMBRIDGE FOR THE YEAR 1885.

BY

THOMAS EDWARD SCRUTTON,

M.A. LL.B. : BARRISTER AT LAW; PROFESSOR OF CONSTITUTIONAL LAW AND
HISTORY IN, AND FELLOW OF, UNIVERSITY COLLEGE, LONDON: LATE
SCHOLAR OF TRINITY COLLEGE, CAMBRIDGE: AUTHOR OF "THE
LAWS OF COPYRIGHT"; "THE INFLUENCE OF THE ROMAN
LAW ON THE LAW OF ENGLAND"; ETC.

"So shall he have the curse of his father, but the land of his
grandfather." BACON.

CAMBRIDGE:
AT THE UNIVERSITY PRESS.
1886

𝕮𝖆𝖒𝖇𝖗𝖎𝖉𝖌𝖊:

PRINTED BY C. J. CLAY, M.A. AND SONS,

AT THE UNIVERSITY PRESS.

TO

KENELM EDWARD DIGBY,

THIS WORK,

WHICH OWES SO MUCH TO HIS WRITINGS,

IS DEDICATED

BY

HIS FORMER PUPIL

THE AUTHOR.

PREFACE.

THE Yorke Prize of the University of Cambridge, to the establishment of which this work owes its existence, was founded about thirteen years ago by Edmund Yorke, late Fellow of St Catharine's College, Cambridge, and, under a scheme of the Court of Chancery, is given annually to that graduate of the University, of not more than seven years' standing from his first degree, who shall be the author of the best essay on some subject relating to the "Law of Property, its Principles, and History in various Ages or Countries." The subject prescribed for the year 1885 by the Adjudicators (Arthur Cohen, Q.C., M.P., and R. Romer, Q.C.), was "The History and Policy of the Laws restraining the Alienation and Settlement of Land in England." The prize was awarded to the Essay bearing the motto : "*Te teneam moriens*," which is now published in accordance with the conditions of the Award.

I am fully conscious that this essay sees the light under serious disadvantages. The subject it deals with has already been so fully treated by Mr Kenelm Digby and Mr Pollock, Mr Kay, Mr Brodrick and Mr Arnold, each from a different point of view, that there can hardly be room for another work on the subject. These pages bear the additional stigma of being a Prize Essay, and it is a commonplace of criticism that from that source no good thing can come. My critics, however, have been so forbearing to two previous trials of their patience in the shape of Prize Essays, that I am sure they will in this case distribute their blame and censure aright. That the Yorke Prize Essay is written at all, the late Mr Edmund Yorke, assisted by the Court of Chancery, must bear the responsibility; that it is written in this year on this particular subject the Adjudicators, and not the author, are the cause; that it is published, is the result of the scheme sanctioned by the Court of Chancery. The author's modesty would prefer to receive the money value of the prize without the additional honours of publicity.

While life is too short to review the reviews of one's work, there is yet one criticism on my last Essay, to which, as it may also affect the present work, I should wish to refer. The *Saturday Review* regretted that my treatise " was marred by a pervading flippancy in tone," and expressed the hope that I might when a little older become "less cocksure." I naturally took this to heart, and was about to endeavour to mould my style on the sober and modest exemplar prescribed by the *Saturday Review* itself. But my intentions were bewildered by a critic in the *Law Quarterly Review*, who informed me that "the author's opinions are for the most part sound and sober, and are clearly and modestly stated." And on reflection I felt that a style which was, in the opinion of two such authorities, both "sober" and "flippant," "cocksure" and "modest," was such a unique production as to be worth preserving.

In the present essay, I do not claim to have done more than collect as carefully, and state as clearly as I could the methods and degrees in which the State has recognized and upheld from time to time the power of the individual to dispose of and control the ownership and management of his land, both during his life and after his death. I have paid especial attention to the earlier periods of the law, and have availed myself freely of the priceless records of Domesday. My indebtedness to Mr

Digby is visible on every page, and I have derived great assistance from the study of Mr Pollock's little book, as exhaustive in matter as it is admirable in exposition. But I have always endeavoured to go straight to the original authorities, and I trust that when Parliament is again at liberty to devote itself to the consideration of English matters, and when the whole question of the Reform of the English land laws is under consideration, this little work will be found of some use, as containing a short but accurate account of the history of those laws.

T. E. S.

1, ESSEX COURT, TEMPLE,
Aug. 3, 1886.

TABLE OF CONTENTS.

INTRODUCTION.

THE history of the English Land Law is a history of intentions of Parliament frustrated by the ingenuity of lawyers, of
national legislation perverted and thwarted in the interests of a
class. The conservative tendencies of the English people have
clung to the forms of a by-gone day, though they have served
but to fetter the modern spirit. The object of the old technicalities has been defeated by fictions of the most cumbrous and
artificial character, which in turn have lingered on in the sanctity
of their antiquity long after their original purpose has been
answered, while their continued existence has only given rise to
expense and uncertainty of title. In the law of England, relics
of the feudal ages, when the land was held by tenures whose
main object was in turbulent times to provide for its safe culture
and for the defence of the nation, have survived, long after the
reason for their existence was dead. In this "Herculaneum
of feudalism," as it has been called, the legal explorer must
still resort to the early centuries of our history to find the
original justification of institutions and rules which have no
longer any but a historical excuse for their survival. The legislation of this century has patched in to the edifice which the
posthumous ambition of landowners has employed the ingenuity
of lawyers to erect, and which the evasiveness of lawyers has
prevented Parliaments, however earnest in the work, from
destroying, modern rules and a modern organization. The Lord
Protector Cromwell's words are still true that the "Law of
England is a tortuous and ungodly jumble."

A law which has developed by fiction and by accident, rather

S.   1

than by direct legislation or clear intent, which has survived
by chance and by conservative instincts, rather than through
foresight and intelligent maintenance, can only be satisfactorily
explained historically.   In the following pages I shall therefore
endeavour to trace the history of the restrictions on the
alienation of and succession to land step by step from the
earliest times.

CHAPTER I.

ANGLO-SAXON LAND LAW.

PROPERTY in land in Anglo-Saxon Law falls under two great classes.

I. *Customary Estates:* the nature and incidents of which depended not on any writing but either on the customary law of the community, or, as in the case of estates of folc-land, on a grant not embodied in writing, together with customary law.

II. Land held by written grant, or *Book-land,* the rights of the owner of which depended not on custom, but on the terms of the Book, or written instrument by which it was conferred.

Customary Estates again were divided into three classes :—
1. *Heir-land,* or *Family Land; Yrfe-land,* or *ethel;* which was owned by individuals[1]. 2. *Community-land,* said to be owned by the community in a Mark, and certainly claimed by the Lord in a Manor, in which the members of the free community, or the *geburs, villani,* and *bordarii* of a manor, had subordinate rights, their relations to their lord or to the community being determined mainly by custom. 3. *Folc-land,* owned by the people or state, from which in turn estates might be granted by parol to individual holders.

The subordinate estates carved out of Customary Land also go by the name of *Laen-land.* Mr Kemble would limit this term to such estates as were held of a lord, but not created by any writing. Mr. Lodge, in his essay on the Anglo-Saxon Land

---

[1] Sometimes called *alod,* as to the correctness of which term see Pollock, *Land Laws,* p. 191. Note B.

Law, calls such estates "*unbooked laens*," and applies the term "*booked laens*" to all subordinate estates of land, carved out of the full property in land and created by writing, thus taking the general term "*laen*" to mean all estates in land where there was a reversion or remainder over from the original grant. Mr Pollock criticizes both the use of the term *laen*, as applied to estates created by book, and also the proposition that estates in *folc-land* were unbooked *laens*; he himself holds *laens* to involve "holding under a definite person or superior by specific services," and as estates of *folc-land* were held from the state, and not from a definite person, he refuses them the name of *laens*[1].

With regard to each of these classes, we have now to consider:

I.   The holder's power of alienating them during his life.

II.   The holder's power of disposing of them on his death, by Will.

III.   The course of Intestate Succession with regard to them.

A.   *Customary Land.*   I.   *Heir-land*[2].

The advocates of the Mark-System allege the division of the land of each community into: 1. the Homestead, in which private property apart from the community was gradually established[3]: 2. Arable lands, which were allotted annually to the members of the community according to customary rules: 3. Pasture and Waste, which were shared by the community in common without any, even temporary, allotment of particular portions. And in the growth of private property in the Homestead, they find the origin of *Heir-land*.

This property at first is that of the family; its nature and incidents are based upon the needs and regulated by the rights of the family: but the family's private property gradually becomes the private property of the individual. There seems little doubt that originally Heir-land, or *yrfe-land*, whatever its

---

[1] *Land Laws*, p. 194.
[2] *Anglo-Saxon Law*, pp. 68—81.
[3] *Suam quisque domum spatio circumdat.* TACITUS.

origin, was inalienable either *inter vivos*, or by Will, and that
the question of intestate succession did not arise with regard to
it; for the family never died, though its members did, while if
it died out entirely, the land would revert to the community.
The next step in its development into private property would
be when the head of the family was recognized as having certain
rights over the land, and we find a stage in the history when
the land is alienable by the head of the family, at first only
within the limits of the family, and with the consent of all the
members of the family. Several instances occur in the charters
where attempts to alienate family land without the consent of
its members failed. Thus, in a charter of Bishop Wulfred [A. D.
811][1], it is recited that Egbert had granted leave to Aldhun to
leave his land by will [*conscribendo dederat*]: *sed post ea Rex
Offa praedictam terram a nostra familia*, [to whom Aldhun had
willed it], *abstulit, videlicet quasi non liceret Ecgberhto agros hereditario jure scribere* (because family land might not be
booked)[2].

Another instance is found in a suit in which Ealdred, Bishop
of Worcester, was concerned. Toki, a King's thegn, had willed
to the bishop land held *"jure haereditariae successionis."* But
his son Aki attacked the will; *"eam terram parentum successione
ad suum jus reclamasset,"* whereupon the bishop compromised
the matter with the king's consent for 8 marks, and Aki gave
him the land, *"liberam a sua et ab omni parentelae.suae haeredi-
taria proclamatione, et scripto firmato reconsignavit, ut libere eam
posset dare seu vendere cuicumque vellet absque ullius contradic-
tione[3]."* In some cases also the kindred join in the grant for
additional security[4], and attempts by kindred to break the

---

[1] Cod. Dip. cxcv.

[2] The reason for a similar interference by Offa with a gift to the
church by Aldhun of land given him
by Egbert, is stated elsewhere to be
"injustum esse quod minister ejus (i.e.
Aldhun), praesumpserit terram sibi
a domino distributam, absque ejus
testimonio in alterius potestatem
dare:" this looks like a grant prohi-

biting alienation without leave of the
king, but it is noticeable that Offa
did not restore the land to Aldhun's
family, who were wronged by his will,
but " suis distribuit ministris." Cod.
Dip. MXX.

[3] C. Dip. DCCCV. *Anglo-Saxon Law,*
App. No. 30.

[4] C. Dip. MXVII.

wills which purport to alienate Heir-land from the family are frequent[1].

On the other hand the celebrated Will of Duke Alfred is written to show "who are the men of my kin and my companions, to whom I will my *yrfe-land*, and my *boc-land*[2]." *Yrfe-land* here is Heir-land, and the possibility of leaving it by will, certainly within the limits of the kindred, and perhaps beyond, is shown. A grant of Offa's runs: "*Duddono meo ministro, et post se homini suae propinquitatis cui ipse relinquat*[3]." In the will of Aethelric he leaves certain land to his mother, with power to alienate it, "*cum recto consilio propinquorum meorum, qui mihi haereditatem dabant*[4]." Beorhtric and Aelfswyth make a will "*testibus his praesentibus de propriis parentibus suis*[5]." Leofwine buys land from Edric his kinsman "aefre *in his cynn* tó fáne and to syllanne ðam ðe him aefre leófost beó[6]." Sellers to Bishop Aelfwold arranged "ðaet hi wurdon sehte ðaet ða gebroðra eallae geeódon of ðám lande, bútan anum," to whom it was bequeathed, and that he should hold it for his day[7].

Development of the incidents of family land seems therefore to be, from absolute inalienability to private ownership within the family, admitting of alienation within the family and by the consent of its members[8]; thence to private ownership and power of alienation outside the family with the consent of the king and Witan, which is substituted for that of the family; and thence to the full power of alienation without any restrictions. An example of this last stage appears, when Wulfred grants to the church "aliquem partem meae *propriae hereditariae terrae*," without any reference to his kin, or to the consent of the king

---

[1] See also Cod. Dip. CLVI., CLXXXVI., CCLVI., the last a very amusing record, in which the church, who were as usual beneficiaries under the will, were attacked by a person whom the reporter describes as "*ille antiquus venenatissimus serpens.*"

[2] C. D. CCCXVII. circa A.D. 880. *Quaere*, whether family land could be left to the "companions," "*gefeora.*"

[3] C. D. CXXXVII. A.D. 779.

[4] C. D. CLXXXVI. A.D. 804.

[5] C. D. MCCXLII. A.D. 962.

[6] C. D. DCCCII. A.D. 1056.

[7] C. D. MCCCXXXIV. A.D. 1046; see also CCXXVIII.

[8] Some traces of this stage may perhaps appear in the customs of some manors, e.g. Millan in Norfolk, where, if any copyholder wishes to sell his land, his kindred have the right of pre-emption in order of nearness of blood. Hazlitt's Blount, p. 221.

and Witan[1]. This is early in date, but it is impossible to assign any strict limits of time to the particular stages suggested above, which varied with each piece of land, and, as is usually the case in changes of customary law, probably overlapped to a considerable extent.

Family-Land thus passes from inalienability to perfect alienability. Wills are introduced by ecclesiastical influence, and frequently used for clerical benefit; the progress is towards freedom of testation, unless the kindred are powerful enough to prevent it. In intestacy the land is divided among all the sons equally, and, failing sons, among all the daughters, this being the custom which survived in socage lands after the Conquest, and which still survives in Kent under the name of Gavelkind. The custom known as Borough-English, the Continental *Jüngsten-Recht*, whereby the youngest son succeeds to the paternal inheritance, also exists in some parts of the country.

The progress of Family-land is thus from a property belonging to the family and inalienable, to a fully alienable property, belonging usually to the head of the family. In this progress the position of the individual is strengthened at the expense of the claims of the family. The most potent influence effecting this change is to be found in the desire of the church to benefit by gifts, or legacies in wills, themselves a clerical introduction.

II. *Community Land* may be regarded from two points of view. In the first place, a certain area of land was owned by an individual, or a family, or a community; in the second place it was tilled by tenants who had customary rights against the owners of the land and amongst themselves. Until recently however it has been an accepted article of faith in England that the early English land-system was one in which the cultivators were themselves the owners, one in which the land was owned by village communities or Marks. The Manor, or form of community where there is but one owner whose land is tilled under customary rules by free and serf tenants, is treated as a later encroachment on this. Indeed Mr Elton confidently assigns the parcelling out of the land into Manors to the reign of

[1] C. D. ccxxv. A.D. 805—831.

Edward the Confessor[1]. But the Bishop of Chester, together
with Dr Gneist, has refused to recognize the Mark as the "basis
of local administration." "It cannot safely be affirmed," says
Dr Stubbs, "that the German settlers in Britain brought with
them the entire system of Mark organization[2]." He indeed
makes the Township his constitutional unit, and represents it,
as we have it in history, "either as a body of allodial owners who
have advanced beyond the stage of land community, retaining
many vestiges of that organization; or a body of tenants of a
lord who regulates them, or allows them to regulate themselves,
on principles derived from the same source[3]." Mr Lodge will
not even accept the Township as the unit of the Constitution, for
he argues that the historical communities were mainly dependent,
or settled on and owned by a lord, as opposed to independent, or
owning the land themselves[4]. This view Mr Seebohm's learned
and original work strongly supports; for he indeed makes an
unexpected attack on the very foundations of the Mark-System,
by showing that the early Swiss communities in which Von
Maurer found his primitive Marks are at least equally capable
of being explained on the hypothesis of manorial communities
holding of an abbey, as their lord[5]. This is not the place to
enter into a discussion as to the origin of manors, but Mr
Seebohm appears to me to prove conclusively the identity of the
manorial communities in their tenures, customs, and services,
with the communities existing before the Conquest, and
undoubtedly holding land in common. And if this is so it is,
to say the least, not improbable that these latter were dependent
communities, settled on land owned by a lord.

The importance of this as bearing on questions of alienation
of, and succession to, land seems to me to be this. Heir-land, as
explained by Lodge and Pollock, arises from the growth of
private property in a village community. Now if this community were independent, the rights of the family and individual
being established as against the rights of the community, freedom of alienation in the individual or family would result.

[1] Elton, *Tenures of Kent*, p. 121.   [4] *Anglo-Saxon Law*, p. 82.
[2] Stubbs, I. 83.   [5] Seebohm, *Village Community*, pp.
[3] Stubbs, I. 85.   328—335.

But if the community were dependent, though the individual tenant might have well-established customary rights against his fellow-tenants, and even against his lord, in his homestead, and though custom might bind the lord to recognize the descent of land to heirs, I do not see how the ordinary manorial tenant could acquire, as against his lord, the right of alienation or of devise. Free tenants added to the Manor might often, as we know from Domesday, "*ire quo voluerunt cum terra*," commend themselves and their land to another lord; though many of them again could only "*ire quo voluerunt*," change their allegiance by abandoning their land, or at the utmost alienate it so that the new tenant should hold of the manor[1]; while others again "*non potuerunt recedere cum terra.*" But I do not think there is any evidence[2] that the ordinary *villani* and *bordarii* at this or any time could alienate without their lord's consent; and this consent was probably more of a reality, when Villein-services had not yet been commuted for money, and when travelling was less common. The modern agricultural labourer now rarely journeys into "foreign parts," as he calls them; his ancestor of Domesday is not likely to have been more active.

But if this is so, the alienable Heir-land of the member of a community is of small importance, and we must look for Heir-land elsewhere. I think it can be found in all the older manorial communities, regarded from the point of view of the Lord. Many of the newer *thegns* and great men derived their land undoubtedly from grants by book from the folc-land, or some few from transfers of *heir-land* by writing: but the older proprietors, I think, held most of their land as Heir-land, which had descended in their family from the original settler to whom had been granted the manorial estate which the conquered were still tilling on the site of the Roman villa, which their former conquerors had abandoned[3]. In these lands, family rights would conflict with the claims of the individual, and in these lands, the growth of

---

[1] Domesday, 140, a. 2, "a vassal of Asgar held this land, and might sell it, but the soke remained in Hitchin."

[2] Except perhaps in Kent: Elton, *Tenures of Kent*, pp. 39, 40.

[3] See Seebohm on the local evidences in Hertfordshire. *V. C.* p. 424 *et seq.*

individual property, set out by Lodge and Pollock, may be traced. This is the class of estate we find in Domesday everywhere in England but in the Eastern and Danish counties, where the original tillers of the soil had disappeared, and the land seems to have been cultivated on a system more akin to a free community, by socmen and *liberi homines*. Here again, we shall find a place for Heir-land, and here the rights of the family will not easily die out. But community-land, in the sense of land which a free community held in tillage, in my opinion filled a very small place in English rural economy. The English communities were dependent on a lord.

Mr Seebohm has suggested[1] that the right of succession to the manorial holding, the equal *yardland* of the *geburs* or *villani*, was to one son only, whether the oldest or youngest, for the equal holdings could have been preserved in no other way. This necessity, he argues, caused the abandonment of gavelkind, or equal division, while the *Jüngsten-Recht*, or Borough English, an old custom of tribal households, survived in some cases to determine which son should be the favoured one. The customs of many manors appear to contradict this theory; and the difficult questions of early manorial customs can hardly be solved till the treasures of history in the Court Rolls of the Manors are brought to light.

III.   The *Folc-land* was the land of the *folc*, or people, and it could only be permanently alienated from them by a grant in writing, or Book, made by their representatives, the King and Witan, when it ceased to be *folc-land*. But there were also estates of *folc-land* concerning which very slight evidence exists, but which appear to have been estates for the grantee's life, reverting to the *folc* on his death. They were certainly not devisable by will, nor were they estates of inheritance, descending in a fixed line on the grantee's death. Duke Alfred's will runs : " I bequeath to Aethelwald my son 3 hides of *boc-land*...and if the King will give him the *folc-land* to the *boc-land*, then he may have and enjoy it, but if it shall not be so, then let my wife give him which she will, either the land at Horsley or that at Langafeld[2]." This shows both that Alfred by himself could not

---

[1] Seebohm, pp. 77, 352.   [2] C. D. cccxvii.

bequeath his estate of *folc-land*, and also that Aethelwald, as his son, would not *eo jure* inherit it. Again Abbot Wulfwold formally recites to the *scirgemot* a grant by the King, as an unfettered estate, "to give or sell during my day or after my day to whomsoever it best pleases me," of land "which my father held[1]." Here the Abbot's father appears to have held an estate of *folc-land*, and the Abbot to have obtained its regrant as unfettered *book-land*. But as from the nature of this tenure no charter existed to record its incidents, it is impossible to speak of it with any certainty. It is probable that the holder of an estate of *folc-land* might alienate his interest in it during his life, in which case the subordinate interest, as held of a definite holder, and not of the State, would be *laen-land*.

B. Land held by the terms of a writing, or Book.

In the case of *Book-land*, from the method of its creation, far more information exists. If created out of *Heir-land*, it would be by a simple charter or book, to which the family, or the King, might at certain stages of its history be parties; if out of *folc-land*, the consent of the King and Witan would be necessary[2]. But the nature of the estate granted followed strictly the terms of the book or charter; and of the various estates so created we have numerous specimens. Book-land probably owed its introduction to the clergy, who monopolized the art of writing, and who were interested in strengthening the power of free alienation and bequest, as against the claims of the family, that they might turn to good use the death-bed repentances of wealthy sinners, by procuring the reversion of their lands to their church or monastery. But even the restrictions in a *book*

---

[1] Circa 1060 A.D. C. D. DCCCXXI. Kemble, *Saxons in England*, I. 300.

[2] Mr Pollock is of opinion that the creations of Book-land out of Heir-land, or Community Land were very slight (*Land Laws*, p. 24). For the reasons just stated, I am inclined to think that more of the Book-land may be derived from alienations of large estates, originally held as Heir-land, than Mr Pollock supposes. The fact that the consent of the King and Witan was obtained to alienations of Heir-land, shows that large estates of that tenure were held, and by great men.

might be disregarded; at least this appears to be the peril guarded against in Alfred's law :—

"The man who has *boc-land* which his kindred left him ; then ordain we that he must not give it from his kindred, if there be writing or witness that it was forbidden by those men who at first acquired it, and by those who gave it to him, that he should do so; and then let that be declared in the presence of the king and the bishop before his kinsmen[1]."

It is difficult to see how this is, as Mr Lodge argues, an attempt to convert *boc-land* into *family-land*; it is rather an attempt to enforce the provisions of the book, for the holder's alienation of his *boc-land* is only to be restrained when such restrictions have been imposed on the land previously. It is curious however that the restriction is spoken of as imposed by "those who first acquired it, or who gave it to him" (these last being presumably the "kindred who left him land" of the earlier part of the law). For we should expect to find the restriction imposed in the original grant to his kindred, whereas it appears to be added to that original grant by the dealings of his kindred with the land. Perhaps this is explained by the addition by will of restrictions on the originally unfettered *boc-land*. It is also curious that the restrictions on alienation can be proved not only by *gewrit*, the book or written will, but also by *gewitnesse*, oral testimony : this may refer either to restrictions on alienation contained in a nuncupative will, or to oral proof of the contents of writings that have been lost.

The possessor of Book-land had powers of alienation, varying with the terms of the book, or will, under which he held. Thus a number of charters give an absolute power of alienation *inter vivos* or by will : e.g.—

"*ita ut quamdiu vixerit potestatem habeat tenendi ac possi-*

---

[1] Laws, § 41. Stubbs, *S. C.* p. 62. *Anglo-Saxon Law*, p. 70. Pollock, *L. L.* p. 194. This law may be compared with the provision in the *Leges Henrici Primi*, an unofficial collection of laws and customs, partly Saxon, partly Norman. "*Si bocland habeat, quam ei parentes dederint, non mittat* *eam extra cognationem suam, sicut praediximus.*" c. LXX. § 21. *Customs of Wessex.* There is no previous reference in the Laws to this, but C. 88 § 14 reads, "*Et nulli liceat foris mittere hereditatem suam de parentela sua, datione vel venditione, sicut diximus, maxime si parentela contradicat.*"

dendi, cuicumque voluerit vel se vivo vel certe post obitum suum relinquendi[1]*.*"

"*ut habeat libertatem commutandi vel donandi in vita sua, et post ejus obitum teneat facultatem relinquendi cuicumque voluerit*[2]*.*"

There are also, to anticipate modern terms, obvious *Estates Tail:* e.g.—

"in jus possessionemque sempiternam sibimet ad habendum quamdiu vivat, suoque relinquendum fratre germano diutius superstes si fuerit......et sic semper in illa sanguinitate paternae generationis, sexuque virili, perpetualiter consistat adscripta[3]."

"Hoc modo donatum est, ut semen masculum possideat et non femininum ; et post obitum prosapiae illius data sit......ad ecclesiam Eofesham[4]": where there is a·species of Estate tail, with remainder to the Church.

We also find estates granted by book for three lives, with a reversion or remainder to some religious foundation[5]: e.g.—
"Ealhferð quanto tempore vixerit, et post se duobus haeredibus, quibus defunctis aecclesiae Weogornensi restituatur": "freolîce his daeg forgeaf, and aefter his daeg twâm yrfeweardum" (heirs) "ðaem ðe sylf wille." One of these books has a note explaining that Aelfward was the first life, and the land was then in the hands of his daughter, who was the second life[6].

The right of alienation was sometimes restricted by a right of pre-emption on the part of the grantor. In an old deed in the Canterbury archives, the Prior of Christchurch grants land thus[7]: "G. tenebit de nobis has terras jure hereditario; et licebit ei de ipsis tanquam de propriis facere quod voluerit, salvo jure et redditu nostro. Ita tamen quod si eas alicui dare voluerit vel

[1] A.D. 736: Kemble, C. D. I. Pref. xxxi.

[2] A.D. 805. Kemble, *ibid.* Two other examples are curious. A.D. 767: "quam is semper possideat, et post se cui voluerit haeredum relinquat." A.D. 805 : "et jure haereditario firmiter fixa permaneat"—where there appears to be some sort of restriction or limitation to the family. Kemble, *ibid.*

[3] A.D. 869 : Kemble, C. D. I. Pref. xxxiii.

[4] A.D. 784 : Kemble, *ibid.*

[5] Anticipations of the leases for lives, so prevalent in the West of England, and now attacked in Mr Broadhurst's Bill.

[6] A.D. 968: Kemble, I. Pref. xxxiv.

[7] Cited by Elton, *Tenures of Kent,* p. 40 note.

vendere, nobis prius hoc indicabit, et nos ad emendum eas proximiores esse debemus."

In face of all these grants, I do not understand how Mr Digby can say: "in the Anglo-Saxon time, there was as a rule perfect freedom of alienation in the case of book-land[1]." The power of alienation must depend in each case on the form of the grant. Every degree of ownership of book-land is found to exist, from complete freedom of alienation, sometimes fettered by a right of preemption in the donor, through lands booked to the kindred, or to male heirs only, to lands booked for a series of lives, with a reversion to the Church. And lands might be confiscated to the donor, if the conditions of the book were not observed. Thus where Cissa had granted to the Church lands for the erection of religious buildings, "*Ini rex eandem terram diripiens reipublicae restituit*" (i.e. the land become folc-land again), "*nondum constructo monasterio in ea, nec ullo admodum oratorio erecto[2].*"

Laen-land, as we have seen, comprises those estates of land held of a definite lord, other than the State, by definite services, not recorded in a writing. It does not necessarily imply a grant for a fixed term, for there is only one such instance, and that a late one, in all the charters[3]. But it would include all grants of land with a reversion to the owner, not made in writing, and would comprise the lands of a manor, both those held by *libere tenentes*, and those held by *geburs* or *villani*. Mr Lodge appears to sacrifice his authorities to logical classification when he speaks of booked and unbooked laens. It is true that there were booked estates in land, with a reversion to the grantor, but so far from being called "*laens*" they are even contrasted with *laens*[4]. Bishop Oswald of Worcester, whose land-grants are very numerous, frequently grants land thus[5]:—"Now there are 3 hides of this land which Oswald booketh to Eadric his thane,...even as he before held them as

---

[1] Digby, *R. P.* 3rd ed. p. 189.

[2] Kemble, *Saxons in England*, I. 304. C. D. XLVI.

[3] C. D. DCCCCXXIV.

[4] There is one apparent exception (C. D. MLXII), where, in a grant by book, the term "gelaeneð" is used.

[5] C. D. DCXVII, DCLI, DCLXXIX ; Kemble, *Saxons in England*, I. 313.

laen-land"; and again "that he may hold it in as large measure for *boc-land*, as he before held it for *laen-land*."

It seems probable that these *laens* could not be alienated *inter vivos*, but that by the terms of the grant they might be bequeathed or limited in a fixed line of succession. A Law of Cnut's provides that if a man holding land of a lord died intestate (which assumes that he could bequeath his land), the land was to be divided among his kin in proper proportions, the lord taking his *heriot*[1]. But Alfred's translation of Augustine indirectly shows the precarious nature of *laen-land*, by illustrating the contrast between this world's turmoil and the heavenly rest by the figure of the man dwelling on *laen-land*, and hoping that his lord would convert it into *boc-land*, *éce yrfe*, permanent inheritance[2].

Collecting these results, which perhaps I state too definitely:—

I. *Alienation inter vivos.* *Heir-land* could not at first be so alienated as to deprive the family of its rights. It might afterwards be alienated by their consent, which was replaced in later times, as the position of the individual improved, by the consent of the Crown. The restrictions on the alienation of Heir-land became in the end practically obsolete.

Community-land could not be alienated by members of the community without the consent of the community, or its lord, and such alienation was probably in reality a surrender and regrant. The lord of a manor could alienate the whole, or part of his manor; for from his point of view the land was either Heir-land, or Book-land, and the customary rights, if any, of his manorial tenants would not prevent his transferring his interest in the land, and jurisdiction over its tenants, to another lord. It is not likely that the question whether the community could alienate all its land ever arose. *Folc-land*, as an estate of land held by a private person, could probably be alienated during life to the extent of the tenant's interest. The power to alienate *Book-land* was determined by the terms of the book, and varied from complete power to its entire absence, though

---

[1] § 71.   [2] Kemble, *S. in E.*, I. 313. Seebohm, *V. C.* 170.

a tendency to disregard the terms of the Book is observable
in the latter part of the period. *Laen-land* could probably not
be alienated, certainly not so as to deprive the grantor of the
services due to him.

II. *Power of bequest.* Testamentary dispositions were
introduced by the clergy from Roman sources, and their object
was usually to benefit the Church.

Heir-land could not, strictly speaking, be devised, though
the right of the family to set aside a will was gradually
weakened, and wills determining the devolution of land
within the family became allowed.

Community-land could not be devised by the community,
which never died; and estates of community-land were
apparently not the subject of devise as of right by the
members of the community who held them, though the consent
of the lord, either in individual cases, or embodied in the
customs of the manor, might allow of such devise. *Book-land*
was specially known as *terra testamentalis;* it was frequently
created by will; but whether it could be devised by its holder
depended in each case on the terms of the book, as booked
estates of inheritance could not be interfered with by the will
of any one tenant under the book. Estates of *folc-land* could
not be directly devised, though the king, by a new grant, could
give effect to the wishes of the late holder.

Laen-land, according to the law of Cnut, could be devised,
but this must have depended in each case on the terms of the
grant.

III. *Succession at death.* The ordinary rule of succession
before the Conquest was that known in later times as descent
in gavelkind or on socage lands, succession to all the sons
equally, and, failing them, to the daughters equally. This
would apply to all lands not held of manors, and to manors
themselves from the lord's point of view. Mr Seebohm argues
that the manorial system of equal and indivisible *yardlands*
could only have been maintained by a rule of descent to a
single successor, fixed either by the custom of the manor, or
the will of the lord[1]. For equal division of each *yardland*

[1] Seebohm, *V. C.* 176—178.

among the late tenant's children would naturally produce inequality of holdings; but in many manorial records after the Conquest this inequality is not found; the *villani* hold, each his equal *yard-land*, and the same manorial holding has been in the same family for centuries. But though in many manors a custom of succession to one son, whether the eldest, or youngest, prevails, and though there are some traces of a custom of primogeniture in particular manors before the Conquest[1], yet there are no traces before the Conquest of any general rule of primogeniture, and after the Conquest there are manors in which the custom of gavelkind descent is found[2].

The rule of primogenitary succession appears to have made no serious inroads on the principle of equal division before the Conquest, though the change was near at hand, and the Domesday Book furnishes good examples of the method in which it would take place. At Covenham in Lincolnshire, on the land of William de Perci, it is recorded that "Chetel and Turver were brothers, and after the death of their father divided the land, yet so that Chetel, performing the King's service, should have aid of his brother Turver[3]." Here Chetel represents the land for the purposes of taxation and personal service, with an understanding that his co-heir assists him. That the representation should become possession, and the understanding of no effect in the eye of the King's Courts, can easily be conjectured. The same county also affords an instance of the breaking down of descent in gavelkind : in the *Clamores*, or disputed claims, we read :—"Tres fratres, Herold et Godevert et Aluric diviserunt dominicam terram patris sui aequaliter et pariliter; solum Herold et Godevert diviserunt socam patris sui sine tertio fratre et aequaliter et pariliter tenuerunt eam tempore Regis Edwardi[4]...de soca 6 bovata...quod praedicti duo fratres aequaliter et pariliter habuerunt socam T. R. E., eo anno quo

[1] Elton, *Tenures of Kent*, p. 106, et post, p. 56.

[2] e.g. Highbury, and Rothley, see Hazlitt's *Blount*, pp. 159, 263.

[3] f. 354, 1, a, For instances of gavel-kind division, see Lincolnshire f. 375, a, 2, between 3 brothers; Gloucestershire, f. 168, b, 2, between 5 brothers.

[4] Usually abbreviated T. R. E.

2

idem rex mortuus est, filii Godevert habebant socam totam, nesciunt qua ratione, utrum vi vel dono patrui sui[1]."

Gavelkind succession we may conclude to have been the rule in Heir-land, and in Book-land and Laen-land, where no special line of succession was prescribed in the grant, probably at any rate in those manorial holdings held by a free tenure on the lord's domain. Estates of Folc-land would revert to the State, and Estates of Book-land and Laen-land, where special provision for the succession was made in the grant, would follow the lines of the grant.

Restrictions on alienation therefore existed chiefly in Heir-land, for the benefit of the family, and in Book-land, as the exercise of proprietary rights in the original owner, to whose power of fixing the succession by book there seem to have been no limits.

In the first instance the order of succession is fixed by customary law, and no power of modifying it by will exists. Wills are introduced by clerical influence and probably for interested motives. The power of fixing the succession by will conflicts with the rights of the family in Heir-land, and the rights of the remainder-man in Book-land. By both it is stoutly resisted, though the family are less successful than the designated heirs in the book. In each case the individual triumphs, in defeating the claims of the family, and in resisting the attempts to set aside his will, as expressed in the book. The book itself is an encroachment on the customary law of succession, but both books and wills are allowed by the State, because tenure by feudal and military services has not yet developed, and it is not yet of importance either to the Crown or to the lord that the land should be in the hands of tenants, who can do their service acceptably. When this stage arrives we shall find that wills which alter the succession to land disappear.

---

[1] i. 875, a, 2. But why Aluric did not take a share of the *soca*, does not appear; the sons of Godevert appear to hold by descent in gavelkind. So in Warwick, i. 241, a, "De Turchil tenent quatuor fratres"...and Gloucestershire. "There are five hides, five brothers held them for five manors, *et pares erant*." Gavelkind descent explains the numerous entries in Domesday of brothers who hold *in paragio:* cf. Wiltshire, ff. 70, b, 2; 72, b, 7; 73, b, 1. Ellis, *Int.* i. 241, n.

There are two minor restraints on alienation, which we may briefly notice; the devotion of land, especially under the Confessor, to religious purposes, and the creation of restraining rights over land by mortgages. Mortgages are naturally found most frequently in the freer counties of England. In Lincolnshire there are some half-dozen entries in Domesday of land *in vadimonium*, and the existence of a mortgage was of course a restraint on the alienation of the land. We find this actually recorded in Hertfordshire, where in a certain manor "a certain woman had 5 virgates of land under Anschil de Wara, and she might sell them, except one virgate, which was mortgaged to Almer for 10s.[1]

Similarly ecclesiastical ownership had a restraining influence on alienation, besides that exercised by the fact that many ecclesiastical lands were held for one life, or at the most three. Lands owned by the church in Domesday show more restraints on alienation than those held either of the King, or of great Lords: the lordship or jurisdiction *"non potest separari ab ecclesia,"* and sometimes it is the tenant who cannot be separated, but is bound to the land. In Wiltshire, of 32 landowners and their land we find the entry "qui tenuerunt T. R. E. non potuerunt ab ecclesia separari." The hundred in Hertfordshire testify that a certain tenant "could not dispose of it from the church, but that after his death it must return to the church[2]." In Wiltshire, "Alwardus tenet tres hidas quas Ulwardus T. R. E. ab Episcopo emit in vita sua tantum ut postea redirent ad firmam episcopi, quia de dominio episcopi erant[3]." Again: "De hac eadem terra tres hidas vendiderat Abbas cuidam Taino T. R. E. ad aetatem trium hominum, et ipse abbas habebat inde servitium et postea debebat redire ad dominium[4]." This church estate for three lives however allowed considerable liberty to its holder, for in the same county there is an entry: "Toti emit eam T. R. E. de Ecclesia Malmesburiense ad aetatem trium hominum, et infra

---

[1] f. 141, a, 2. Sometimes the mort-gagee had the power to sell—cf. the entry " an Englishman held this land in mortgage, and might sell it"—f. 133, a, 2.
[2] f. 139, a, 2.
[3] f. 66, a, 1.
[4] f. 66, b, 1.

hunc terminum poterat ire cum ea ad quem vellet dominum[1]."
Here the church had not even the *soc* during this term of lives;
but no similar entry occurs in the rest of Domesday. More restricted estates are common: e.g. "Aluric tenuit de Abbatissa
unam hidam...ea conditione ut post mortem ejus rediret ad
ecclesiam, quia de dominica firma erat[2]." Sometimes the church
had not to wait till the death of the holder, but could exert its
influence before: e.g. "Hanc terram reddidit sponte sua ecclesiae Hardingus, qui in vita sua per conventionem debebat
tenere[3]." In Essex a landowner "non potuit vendere sine licentia
abbatis[4]:" and this sometimes affected superior landowners.
Asgar held T. R. E. a manor in Buckinghamshire of the Church
at Canterbury, "so that it could not be separated from the
church[5]," and Archbishop Stigand himself is recorded as having
held land which he could not separate from the church[6]. From
an entry in Cambridgeshire "T. R. E. de hoc manerio tenuit
Ailbertus vi hidas, ita quod non potest vendere nec ab ecclesia
separare, sed post mortem suam restitueretur ecclesiae de Ely[7],"
where *vendere* is contrasted with *separare ab ecclesia*, I should
infer that the latter phrase referred merely to the soke or jurisdiction, and allowed by itself a substitution of another tenant to
the estate which the alienor held of the church.

There are a large number of instances in Domesday of lands
held by the church or private persons on condition of praying
for the donor, or in *frankalmoign*, which of course could not be
alienated by their holders[8]. In Hertfordshire certain lands
"were of the alms of King Edward, and of all the Kings his
forerunners[9]." In Bedfordshire, Alurin a priest held T. R. E.—
one sixth of a hide: "Rex Willielmus sibi postea in eleemosina
concessit, unde pro anima regis et reginae omni ebdomada feria
duas missas persolvit." In Norfolk, "unus liber homo tenet XL
acras terrae in eleemosina et cantat unaquaque ebdomada tres
missas."

[1] f. 72, a, 1.
[2] f. 67, b, 2.
[3] f. 67, b, 1.
[4] So also in Hertfordshire, f. 141, b, 1.
[5] f. 143, b, 2.
[6] f. 135, b, 2.
[7] f. 201, b. See also 202.
[8] Collected by Ellis. Introduction to Domesday, I. 258—260.
[9] f. 141, b, 2.

In lands devoted to religious purposes we inevitably find restrictions on alienation, the multiplication of which leads in the course of time to prohibitions of alienation for such purposes.

Another alleged restriction on alienation before the Conquest may be briefly noticed. Mr Coote has argued that "no land before the Conquest could be alienated without the leave of the King[1]." In support of this startling proposition, he adduces some dozen charters in the *Codex Diplomaticus* in which the gift is recited to be made by the leave of the king. But we have seen that at a certain stage in the history of Heir-land the consent of the king and witan was obtained to its alienation in order to defeat the claims of the family; and it is also probable that many of the greater proprietors made their grants of book-land in the *shiremoot*, or in the *witan*, after the fashion of Private Acts of Parliament, as Mr Pollock suggests, and to obtain greater security for and witness of their alienations. These two causes are quite sufficient to account for the instances Mr Coote cites, without having recourse to the fact that many grants of land contain no such recital of the leave of the King. But Mr Coote's examples explain themselves. Without a minute examination of all, the very first he cites, runs thus: "cum licentia et permissione regis Offani, nos tres germani, uno patre editi, donabimus tibi, Headda abbas, terram juris nostri... nunquam nos haeredesque nostros ullo tempore contra hanc donationem esse venturos[2]"... which is clearly a grant of family land by the brothers who owned it, with the king's leave obtained to bar the claims of the family. And a similar explanation can be given of Mr Coote's other examples. His theory of the necessity of the king's leave for alienation may therefore be dismissed.

With regard to the methods and formalities of alienation there are undoubted instances where a grant was made by Book, and a symbolical transfer was also performed[3]. Thus in

---

[1] *Neglected Fact in English History*, pp. 23, 173. *Romans in Britain*, pp. 247—251.

[2] A.D. 759. *Cod. D.* cv. I. 128.

[3] *Cod. D.* Nos. 12, 104, 114, 1019:

Nos. 114, 177 are marked by Kemble as forgeries, but the incident may have been copied from genuine charters. *Black Book of Peterborough*, ed. Stubbs. Pollock, *Land Laws*, 193.

the eighth century Ethelred, on a visit to Medesham, gave to the brethren he found there 30 *manentes*, and confirmed the gift by placing on the Gospels' Book a sod taken from the place. Again a purchase of lands from the king was ratified in the king's chamber by placing a sod from the land on the Gospels' Book in the presence of the bishop. This symbolism might well find no record in the books, but would play a prominent part in transfers of Heir-land and manorial holdings under the old customary law, where its dramatic character would impress the memory of the witnesses. And the customs still existing in manors of symbolical transfer, as by a straw at Wintringham in Lincolnshire, or by a rod in some of the Norfolk manors, have probably the same origin.

CHAPTER II.

THE EVIDENCE OF DOMESDAY BOOK.

THE question remains to what extent the land of England was held under one or other of these tenures. We fortunately have in Domesday Book an exhaustive enumeration of the classes into which the landowners and cultivators of England fell 20 years after the Conquest. The land was then held and tilled as follows[1]:—

I. *Greater Landowners*	Tenants in Capite	1,400		9,271
	Under Tenants	7,871		
II. *Socage Tenants*	Sochmanni	23,072		36,739
	Dimidii Sochmanni	18		
	Liberi Homines	10,097		
	Liberi Homines Commendati	2,041		
	„ „ Dimidii . .	224		
	Homines	1,287		
III. *Manorial Tenants by servile Tenure*	Villani	108,407		199,568
	„ dimidii	49	110,125	
	[2]Buri	62		
	Coliberti	858		
	Bovarii	749		
	Bordarii	82,119	82,624	
	„ dimidii	15		
	„ pauperes	490		
	Cottarii	5,054	6,819	
	[3]Coscets	1,749		
	Coterii	16		
IV. Slaves	Servi			25,156
				270,734

[1] Ellis, *Int.* II. 511.
[2] Apparently relics of the *geburs* of the *Rectitudines.* Thorpe, *Institutes,*
pp. 186, 187.
[3] Obviously the *Cotsetle* of the *Rec-titudines.*

Out of the 283,242 persons enumerated in Domesday, over 270,000 are thus accounted for, the balance being composed of *Burgenses*, 7968; tradesmen and artizans, as *presbyteri*, 994, *ancillae*, 467, *salinarii*, 108, *porcarii*, 427, *fabri*, 64, etc., and foreigners; *Francigenae*, etc. 352, *Walenses*, 111.

At the time of Domesday, therefore, the land of England can be ·looked at under two aspects: I. The 9271 greater land-owners, holding of the king or of tenants in chief, who between them held together with the king nearly all the cultivated land in the country; the greater part of this land was in manors, each divided into two parts, the lord's domain, and the land held in villeinage by the copyhold tenants of the manor. II. From the second point of view, all this land was cultivated by the socage and villein tenants, in all some 236,307 men. The majority of the former held manorially by free tenure, the latter manorially by servile tenure, and the villein tenants in addition cultivated much of the domain land by the work they owed to the lord. Nearly all the occupied land in the kingdom would therefore have to be considered under two heads: I. The rights of alienation and succession as possessed by its lords. II. Those rights as possessed by its cultivators.

Now if we look at the land-system before the Conquest the same double aspect is presented: the land as held after the Conquest by the 9000 feudal landowners was probably held before the Conquest by nobles and thegns as Heir-land or Book-land, Heir-land being the older form of holding, while some slight portion was in estates of Folc-land and laen-land. No settled forms of feudal tenure existed though much of the book-land was held with a reversion to the donor, and in the reign of Edward the Confessor there are the germs of feudalism: e.g. "Godwin comes tenuit B. de rege Edwardo sicut Allodium[1]." The Con-queror gives to the Abbey of Westminster the manor of Everslea "cum omnibus rebus et consuetudinibus et legibus sicut quatuor socmanni de Edwardo rege pro iii maneriis in Allodio libere tenuerunt[2]." The meaning of the term *allodium* as used in Domesday is not quite certain; in later times it is used to

---

[1] f. 22, b, and other instances, see Ellis, i. 54—56.   [2] Cotton MS. cited Ellis, i. 56, n.

translate "Book-land," a word which only occurs once in Domesday[1]. The term occurs most often in Sussex, where more than
80 landowners are described as *allodiarii*, or as holding land
T. R. E. *per allodium*, in many cases as a manor. These entries
are not scattered over the county, but occur in batches in— —
particular localities. The term probably signifies an estate
either of Heir-land or of *Boc-land*, with a power of alienation and
devise then unfettered. Its freedom is shown by the constant
Sussex entry "*nunquam geldavit*," showing the free estate, as
compared with the entry "*geldavit*" in a serf county like Wiltshire.

Looked at from above therefore we have the superior landowners with their grants and alienations of land, their wills and
charters, filling the *Codex Diplomaticus*, which however from the
nature of the tenures is almost entirely confined to transactions
in Book-land, the mass of Heir-land changing hands without any
formal records surviving. And these grants usually, by the
boundaries of the land granted, clearly show that a community
in form manorial was settled on the land[2].

Looked at from the inferior side we have the numerically
important class of *geburs*, or *villani*, and *bordarii*, whose services
and position are depicted in the *Rectitudines Singularum
Personarum*[3]. At the time of Domesday, it is estimated that 2¼
million acres out of 5,000,000 in cultivation were tilled by this
class, and that the lord's demesne, for which they furnished
much of the labour, would account for another two million acres,
leaving some 750,000 acres to be tilled by the *sochmanni* and
libere tenentes. Now it is certain that after the Conquest the
socmen and *libere tenentes* are in the vast majority of instances
the free tenants of the manor, usually holding portions of the
lord's demesne, or tilling land reclaimed from the lord's waste.
And these *libere tenentes* may often hold other land on the
manor by villein or servile tenure. The explanation of their
existence appears to me to depend on two causes. First they
represent smaller freeholders whom weakness and the growth

---

[1] "quod tenuerunt duo liberi homines de Rege Edwardo in bochelande."
Larkins, *Domesday of Kent*, p. 45, l. 21.

[2] Seebohm, *V. C.*, pp. 127, 128.

[3] Thorpe, *Institutes*, pp. 186, 187.

of feudal tendencies have led to commend themselves to a lord, and receive land, which would naturally be on his demesne, from him to cultivate by a free tenure. That this is so is shown by the striking fact that the *sochmanni* and *liberi homines* in Domesday are found almost entirely in the Danish districts of England[1]. Now the Danish settlers with their customs of freedom preserved in their districts individual independence, as opposed to dependence on a lord, longer than the rest of England. It is not therefore surprising that these districts should be found to be the stronghold of small landowners at the time of Domesday; and we may take it that the *sochmanni* and *libere tenentes* of Domesday represent the last of the smaller landowners, who held out as allodial and independent proprietors.

Undoubtedly much of this change of the smaller landholders into men under the protection of a lord, and the absorption of the land which they had held in free tenure into the manor of their lord, took place immediately after the Conquest, for we have the process recorded in numerous entries in Domesday. At Haddiscoe in Norfolk we see the process of commendation: "hic sochmannus commendavit se Alwino tempore Wilhelmi regis, et erat inde saisitus quando rex dedit terram Rogero Bigoto." In Gloucestershire, "they who held these lands in King Edward's time put themselves and their lands under the protection of Brihtric[3]." At Bedfont in Middlesex " three sokemen did not belong to the manor in King Edward's time[3]." At Tring in Hertfordshire we have a very full account[4]: " Engelric held this manor in the time of King Edward, and there were two sokemen there, vassals of Osulf; they held two hides and might sell them :

---

[1] Percentage of socmen and free men to population.

Lincolnshire	45	per cent.
Suffolk	40	,, ,,
Norfolk	32	,, ,,
Derby	28	,, ,,
Notts	27	,, ,,
Northampton	13	,, ,,
Essex	5	,, ,,

The first 5 being strongly Danish and

East Anglian. In no other county are more than 4 per cent. recorded; they are only present in 12 other counties, in 9 of which they are 1 per cent., or less, of population. In 14 counties they are entirely absent.

[2] 163, b, 2.

[3] 130, a, 1.

[4] 137, a, 2.

the same Engelric laid these sokemen to this manor after the
coming of King William; and a vassal of the Abbot of Ramsey's
had 5 hides of this manor after the same manner. He could
not give or sell this land from the church of St Benedict: and
this land Engelric laid to the manor after the coming of King
William, which land was not there in the time of King Edward,
as the hundred affirm. Those aforesaid three sokemen, who are
now there having one hide, were vassals of Engelric and might
sell their land." This instance shows three stages in the
position of the socmen. At first, T. R. E. two of them held
their land as their own, with free liberty of alienation, but for
protection had commended their persons to Osulf; the third
had commended himself to the Abbot of Ramsey, and could not
alienate his land, so that the soc or jurisdiction passed from the
church of St Benedict at Ramsey[1]. After the Conquest the
second stage begins. Engelric, who held the manor of Tring,
joined these socmen and their land to the manor; the first two
changed their personal lord, but might sell their land, though
probably, as in so many other cases, the *soc* would remain in
Tring. The third socman had also changed his lord; how the
soc of his land, if it was in the Abbey of Ramsey, was transferred
to Engelric, we are not told: but he could then sell his land,
subject, I presume, to the same restriction as the others.
Lastly, at the time of Domesday, Earl Eustace held the manor;
the three socmen could sell their land and leave the manor, but
the purchasers of the land would become tenants of the manor
under the earl. Their holdings of land have decreased from 7
hides to 3[2].

[1] This I think is the explanation of
the clause; but it may be that the
reversion of the land was in the church,
in which case it is curious that it
should become part of the manor, but
such a case is recorded in the same
county, f. 137, a, 1: "Godwin held this
land of the church of St Peter; he
could not sell it, but after his death it
ought to revert to the church, as the
hundred testify; but his wife *vertit se
per vim cum hac terra* to Edith the
Fair, and held it in the day on which
King Edward died."

[2] There is a similar example at Thetchworth in the same county, where "five
sokemen [all of them vassals of a lord] held this manor, nullus eorum ad ante-
cessorem Wigot pertinuit sed unusquisque terram suam vendere potuit. Horum
unus terram emit a Wilhelmo rege novem uncias auri, postea ad Wigot se vertit

Our conclusion is therefore that the further we get back from the Conquest, the more of these smaller landholders shall we find surviving as freeholders, independent of any lord or manor, who have not yet fallen into dependence by commendation. And this is important to our subject because the Domesday references to such owners show that many of them were free to alienate or bequeath without their lord's consent. Thus at Stamford in Lincolnshire 77 socmen "habent terras suas in dominio, et petunt dominos ubi volunt[1]." "Potuit ire cum terra quo volebat" is a common phrase in Domesday, of tenants who could commend themselves and their

[1] Ellis, I. 70. f. 336, b, 2.

pro protectione[a]. Here one of the sokemen who had commended their persons, but whose land was free, first bought his land of the King, or redeemed it from forfeiture, and then, finding this insufficient, attached himself and, I suppose his land, to Wigot, lord of the manor. In the same county (f. 138, a, 2) "a sokeman, one of the men of Anschil de Wara, had there one virgate, and might sell it; and after the coming of King William it was sold, and added to the manor, where it was not in King Edward's time[b]." In the same place William, a vassal of the lord of the manor, "invasit terram suam supra regem, sed reclamat dominum suum ad protectionem." Again, "There is one sokeman who was not in the manor T.R.E.: he has one hide, he was a vassal of Queen Edith T.R.E. and he might sell his land" (f. 139, b, 1). Ilbert the sheriff joined 7 sokemen of King Edward's and two vassals of private lords to the manor "who were not there T.R.E." (f. 142, a, 1). In Buckinghamshire, "In this manor two sokemen hold 1½ hides; it laid not there T.R.E." (f. 143, a, 1).

In Essex we see the process going further: "There was T.R.E. a certain liber homo holding half a hide, *who has now been made one of the villeins[c].*" Some of the freemen who survive the Conquest are in a very anomalous position. In Kent[d], "in hoc manerio tenet unus homo, nec pertinet ad illum manerium, neque potuit habere dominum praeter regem." In Wiltshire, "unus tainus T.R.E. poterat ire ad quem vellet dominum, et T.R.W. sponte se vertit ad Ernulfum," of whom he now holds[e]. In Essex there was a *liber homo* "who paid soc to the manor, and yet he could go with his land where he wished:" "To this manor were added 15 acres T.R.W., which were held by one freeman T.R.E." In this county Engelric immediately after the Conquest is recorded as having "seized" a number of socmen and added them to his manors, while near Sudbury 137 socmen were transferred to the domain land of Richard, which they continued to till. How slight the tie of personal allegiance was, as compared with the tie of land tenure, is shown by a record in the same county of Coleman, a vassal of Wigorn's T.R.E. "who was so free that he would go with his land and soc where he wished[f]."

[a] f. 137, b, 2.
[b] See also two sokemen at Ware, 138, b, 2.
[c] f. 1, b.
[d] Larkins, p. 22, l. 9.
[e] f. 70, a, 2.
[f] f. 40, b.

land to another lord; this would not apply where the lord had granted the land originally, the phrase being then *"potuit ire quolibet."*

Again the customs of many manors show that reclamation of waste land was one of the means by which an Englishman before the Conquest might raise his position in life. That it was so with the higher class of thegns we know from King Alfred's selections from Augustine[1]. "It pleaseth every man," he says, "when he has built himself a cottage upon his lord's *laen* with his assistance, to take up his rest thereon, and provide for himself upon the *laen* until some day through his lord's grace he may obtain boc-land and permanent inheritance." The settler might clear and till a place in the forest as a *laen* in the hope of obtaining from the lord a permanent and secure tenure of inheritance. That villeins in manors improved their position thus may be illustrated by the tenures in several of the Sussex manors[2], where the land of the manor is divided into Bond-land, which is also called yard-land, the ordinary copyhold tenure, and Soc-land. This latter is clearly derived from the estates of *socmanni* or *liberi tenentes* in the lord's demesne, and one of the modes of its creation is shown by the fact that it is also called *"Assart* Land," which signifies "cleared," while the customs of the manor contemplate that a villein tenant may hold Assart-land as well as Bond-land.

In any attempt however to speak positively as to the extent to which alienation is 'prevalent or possible in the Anglo-Saxon land system, great confusion is caused by the fact that the same land may bear various characters. Thus the king may have granted out of the *folc-land* an estate by book to one of his thegns, with succession to his heirs male. The thegn may cultivate that land by what is practically a manorial community of *villeins* or *geburs*, who cannot alienate their land without his consent, but have customary rights as against each other and their lord, to homesteads in permanence, and temporary allotments of arable land. There may also be on the

---

[1] Kemble, *S. in E.* I. 313. Seebohm, *V. C.* 170.

[2] e.g. Wadhurst, Framfield, Rother-field, Warbleton, etc. Sussex Archaeological Collections, VI. 175, 176.

lord's domain tenants holding in free socage, some of whom have joined their land to the manor, but can transfer both it and their personal allegiance to some other manor at will[1]: others who can sell their land, the jurisdiction remaining in the manor[2]: others again who cannot sell, or even leave their land without the permission of their lords[3]: while, over all their heads, the lordship of the manor cannot be alienated, but passes in the line of succession limited in the Book.

And an investigation of Domesday shows *socmanni* and *libere tenentes* with every degree of power of alienation. Frequently socmen who are in the same manor under the Conqueror, in the time of Edward held by entirely different tenures. In Cambridgeshire on the Manor of Cottenham[4]: "Hanc terram T. R. E. tenuerunt tres sochmanni, horum unus homo S. Ethelredae tenuit tres hidas, et non potuit dare, quae erat de dominio ecclesiae; alter homo abbatis i hidam habuit, et dare potuit sine soca; tertius homo et dare et vendere potest." Here one could not alienate; one could alienate but could not destroy the jurisdiction of the Abbots of Ely over the land; the third had free power of alienation. In another Cambridge manor, we find the entry: "hoc manerium tenuerunt T. R. E. vi sochmanni horum unus homo Eddeue habuit...et recedere potuit; alii homines abbatis de Ely fuerunt...quatuor terram suam vendere potuerunt, soca remansit abbati, et quintus habuit, et recedere non potuit[5]." Here the first could leave his land but not sell it, the last was bound to the land, and the other four can sell their land but the *soc* will remain in the Abbot of Ely[6].

---

[1] *potuit ire quolibet cum terra sua.*   *licentia domini.*

[2] *potuit ire quo voluit.*   [4] f. 201, b, 1.

[3] *non potuit vendere vel recedere, sine*   [5] f. 201, a, 2.

[6] Hertfordshire supplies a large number of varying tenures of socmen: "Asgar the staller held the manor of Sawbridgeworth and there were 4 sokemen there; 2 of them, vassals of Asgar, held half a hide and might sell it except the soke; the third and fourth were vassals of Harold and of Alwin, and might sell and give their land. The soke was Asgar's, and one sokeman, a vassal of Asgar's, had besides two hides, but he could not sell them[a].

"Of this manor Elmer held 4 hides for one manor. Here there were four sokemen; one held half a hide and might sell it. Another held one virgate, but

[a] f. 139, b, 2.

As lands within the same manor may be subject to varying powers of alienation, it naturally follows that the same land-holder may have varying powers of alienation over different portions of his land. Thus in Hertfordshire "Alward held two hides and 3 virgates in Box, he could only sell 3 virgates — of it[1]," and "William holds a hide and a half of the bishop, he might sell the half-hide, but the hide he could not sell without the bishop's leave[2]."

A further confusion is introduced by the fact that the position of landowners and tenants with regard to alienation varies very much in different parts of England. In the Danish counties, where *socmanni* and *liberi homines* were numerous, and where the traditions of freedom and individual independence were strong, liberty of alienation was far more extensive than in the west, where serfs of British origin did much of the agricultural work. Thus in the whole of the county of

---

[1] f. 138, b, 2.   [2] f. 133, b, 2.

could not sell it without the leave of Elmer his lord. The third and fourth had half a hide and might sell it. King Edward had sac and soke over these two. The four were the *homines* of Elmer[a].

Archbishop Stigand held a manor in which "were 6 sokemen, vassals of the Archbishop, and everyone had one hide ; they might sell them except the soke ; but one of them could also sell the soke with his land[b]. Leman, a vassal of the Archbishop, held this land and might sell it, and duo, sokmanni qui ibidem sunt, held three virgates, but they could not sell without the Archbishop's leave[c].

In Greenford in Middlesex, of two sokemen, unus potuit facere quod voluit, unus non potuit dare sine licentia domini[d].

In Cambridgeshire, the socmen were still more fettered in alienation: "quidam socmannus Guert comitis non potuit recedere nec vendere:" "duo sochmanni non potuerunt recedere ab eo manerio." T. R. E. hanc terram tenuerunt quatuor socmanni, homines Waltheof comitis, horum duo tenuerunt unam hidam, recedere sine licentia ejus non potuerunt, alii duo dare et vendere potuerunt[e].

Hertfordshire affords a good instance of the way in which land might be changed from manor to manor: "one sokeman holds eight acres of Geoffrey in Wickham...he himself held it T. R. E., he was a vassal of Godred's, and he could sell it. It was of the king's soke. In T. R. E. it lay in Wickham, Geoffrey placed this soke in Thorey where it was not T. R. E.[f]"

[a] f. 141, a, 1.   [b] f. 142, b, 2.   [c] f. 138, a, 2.
[d] f. 129, b, 1.   [e] f. 201, b.   [f] f. 140, a, 1.

Nottingham, a Danish county[1], the Domesday record of the condition of the lands T. R. E. contains no notice of any restraint on alienation, and, a fact which is more significant when we compare the county with such counties as Hertfordshire, no express statement that any landowner is at liberty to alienate. In Lincolnshire[2], the county showing the largest proportion of *socmanni* and *liberi homines*, there are only two entries concerning freedom of alienation or the reverse[3]. The prevalence of free landowners is also shown by the number of entries of mortgages of land[4], entries which are absent as we get further west in Domesday. But on the other hand, in such a county Heir-land would remain in full vigour, and alienation might be restricted from this cause.

Lincolnshire also contains a curious example of *laen-land*, similar to a yearly tenancy, and interesting from its connexion with an historical character. The men of the county say that certain land "fuisse dominicam firmam monachorum: Ulchel abbatem commodasse eam ad firmam Herewardo sicut inter eos

[1] *Nottinghamshire*: Ellis, ii. 476.

Domesday population		5,686
tenants in capite under tenants.	}	188
socmanni		1,516
villani		2,603
bordarii		1,101
servi		26
burgenses		176

[2] *Lincolnshire*: Ellis, ii. 465.

Domesday population		25,305
tenants in capite and under tenants	}	506
socmanni		11,503
villani		7,723
bordarii		4,024
servi		0
burgenses		1,329

[3] *Note*, viz., one as to burgesses of Stamford: "In his custodiis sunt 77 mansiones socmannorum, qui habent terras suas in dominio, et qui petunt dominos ubi volunt, supra quos rex nihil aliud habet nisi emendationem forisfacturae eorum et heriete et thelo-neum," f. 336, b, 2; one as to the *Free Manor* of Hacam [*quaere* an independent community: cf. "free soke," ff. 368, b, 1; and "habebat *tria maneria in propria libertate* de rege Edwardo, f. 376, b, 1]. This entry, after an enumeration like an ordinary manor, continues "In hac villa habuit Robertus presbyter i carucatam terrae de rege in eleemosina et modo cum eadem terra effectus est monachus in Sancta Maria Stow. *Sed non licet terram alicui habere nisi regis concessu.*" [f. 345, 1, a].

Here it seems that as Robert's land was granted by the King in alms, the King's consent is necessary for anyone to hold it. I suppose St Mary of Stow had some rights over the land, as Robertus became a monk there *cum ea terra*. If the entry referred to all land in the manor, it would come earlier.

[4] ff. 367, a, 2; 377, a, 2, etc.

conveniret unoquoque anno, sed Abbas resaisivit eam antequam Herewardus de patria fugeret, eo quod conventionem non tenuisset[1]."

In a less Danish county, Hertfordshire[2], in which there is only one per cent. of *socmanni* and *liberi homines* as against — — 86 per cent. of *villani* and *bordarii*[3], we find entries of powers of alienation constant: some 50 tenants of church land have the entry "*et potuit vendere*," and in the lands held by lay tenants in chief, some 60 tenants may sell their *terra*, while of some 25 it is said "*tenuit hoc manerium et potuit vendere*[4]." There are many entries of church tenants who cannot separate their lands from the church, and of lay tenants who cannot separate the soke of their land from some manor, usually either Hitchin or Tring. Some church tenants cannot sell without the leave of the church, nor some lay tenants without the leave of their lord. Some church tenants, though sokemen, could not sell at all[5]; whilst on the other hand some sokemen could sell the soke with their land. The powers of alienation possessed by nearly every free landowner except the tenants in capite T. R. E. are stated, and I should infer from this fact that the county was in a transition state from the freedom of the older and Danish shires to the servile holdings of the western counties.

In Essex[6], a very common holding is: "non potuit vendere

[1] f. 377, a, 2.

[2] *Hertfordshire.* Ellis, II. 456.
Domesday population . . 4,927
tenants and under tenants 239
socmanni ⎫
liberi homines ⎭ · · · · 49
villani . . . . ., . . . 1,830
bordarii 1,107
cotarii 837
servi 550

[3] As compared with Lincolnshire with 35 per cent. socmanni, and 46 per cent. villani and bordarii.

[4] I cannot discover any distinction between these two entries to explain why one should be used and not the other. Anyone curious in the matter may test his theory by explaining the difference between the two holdings of

Derman in Bradewater Hundred (f. 142, a, 2), at Wodetone and Walchra; of which the two phrases are used. It is true that Walchra is called *manerium*, but from the description of Wodetone, which has demesne, villani, bordarii, and is held of the King, it is clear that it too was a manor.

[5] f. 138, a, 1.

[6] *Essex.* Ellis, II. 441.
Domesday population . . 16,060
tenants and under tenants 615
sochemanni ⎫
liberi homines ⎭ · · · 834
villani 4,087
bordarii 8,052
servi 1,768
burgenses 601

sine licentia domini"; sometimes varied where the person also is bound by "non potuit recedere sine licentia domini." Many *socmanni* are bound in this way: e.g. "XII socmanni qui non recedere potuerunt de terra sua," and a number of socmen T. R. E. are recorded as forcibly added to manors T. R. W. The large number of *bordarii* and *servi* show a population in considerable dependence, which is curious when we consider the early settlement of Essex, and its proximity to the Danish counties.

In Sussex[1] a far freer state of things is found to exist T. R. E., though the county is not uniformly free, and at the time of Domesday there is an entire absence of free tenants of a manor. But we find constant entries of allodial tenure T. R. E. More than 80 then tenants of land are spoken of as *allodiarii*, or holding *per allodium*, followed by the significant *free* entry "*nunquam geldavit*": there are 35 tenants, *qui potuerunt ire quolibet*, and 5 more who could carry their land with them[2]. Entries of restriction, e.g. "Wenestan tenuit de Oswardo, nec quolibet ire potuit," are very scarce, and I should infer that freedom of alienation was the rule in the county before the Conquest, and that most of the minor free tenants found death or the forfeiture of their lands at Hastings.

Kent[3] gives curious results, for Kent is the county in which the old Saxon custom of equal division in intestacy has survived: the "yeoman of Kent with his yearly rent" is well known in English ballads, and, for prose, the Law Courts of the fourteenth century laid down that there was no villeinage in Kent, and that a man's freedom was established by showing that any one of his ancestors was born in Kent[4]. But Domesday

---

[1] *Sussex.* Ellis, II. 496.
Domesday population . 10,410
tenants and under tenants . 549
villani 5,898
bordarii 2,497
cotarii 765
servi 420
burgenses 260
[2] potuit ire quolibet cum terra sua.
[3] *Kent.* Ellis, II. 459.

Domesday population . 12,205
tenants and under tenants . 225
socmen 44
villani 6,597
bordarii 3,118
cotarii 364
servi 1,148
burgenses 661
[4] Pollock, p. 206. Y. B. 30 and 31 Edw. I. 168.

shows a large number of manors; five-sixths of the population
are manorial tenants, and there is a fair proportion of slaves.
There are very few entries respecting powers of alienation in
the Domesday of Kent, and those found relate to freedom of
alienation, which we should therefore infer to be the exception.
Four tenants *potuerunt ire quolibet cum terra*, and four *potuerunt
se vertere quolibet cum terra*, six *potuerunt se vertere quolibet*, one
qui potuit ire quolibet, and one *qui potuit ire quolibet sine licentia
domini*. There are no entries of the simple power of sale, or of
any other restrictions on it. In fact it is not very easy to draw
any inferences as to the condition of the county before the
Conquest, or to see any reason for the exceptional survival of
the old customs after it[1].

Travelling west, we find a state of things distinctly less free.
In Wiltshire[2], which has a large proportion of slaves, and an
entire absence of *socmen* and *liberi homines*, the records as to
alienation are usually merely entries that the tenant *potuit ire
quo voluit;* that he had liberty to take his land with him is
never recorded. There are a large number of church leases, and
over 30 entries "qui tenuerunt T. R. E. non poterant ab
ecclesia separari"; while the constant statement *geldabat* shows
the servile nature of the tenures and the probable absence of
power to alienate the land.

These examples show the complexity of the Anglo-Saxon
land system, especially in the reign of the Confessor, at a time
when the germs of feudalism were developing, and the piety of
the monarch was fettering much of the land with religious
services. Powers of alienation and devise, and the order of
succession, were different according to the character of the land,
the mode in which it was acquired, or even the county in which
it was situated. Lands in the same manor or hundred might
have different qualities, and lands of the same owner might be

---

[1] *v. sub.* pp. 60 et seq.
[2] *Wiltshire.* Ellis, II. 501.
Domesday population . 10,150
Tenants in chief and)
   under tenants   }   .   442
villani 3,049

bordarii 2,754
cottarii 1,697
coliberti 260
servi 1,539
burgenses 295

in his power to a different degree. The restraints which existed on alienation were either in the interests of the family as in heir-land, of the will of the donor as in book-land, of the church, or of the lord or possessor of the *soc* or jurisdiction. Against the first two of these the interests of the individual tenant for the time being were successfully struggling. Restraints imposed for the two latter causes, and especially those created in the interests of the lord, grew to such an extent that they strongly fettered most of the land in England.

CHAPTER III.

ALTHOUGH the germs from which a feudal system, or one in which the organization of society is based upon the tenure of land, might develope certainly existed in England before the Conquest, the Feudal System as it grew in England after the coming of William was undoubtedly of Norman introduction. The essential features of feudalism are tenure of land by each landowner of a superior to whom he is bound by a tie of personal fealty, from whom he receives protection and security, and to whom he owes services, usually military, as the consideration for his enjoyment of the land. The English system shows in addition a personal tie of fidelity to the king as supreme landowner, which overrides the vassal's fealty to his immediate lord, and which tends to counteract the disruptive effects of the continental feudalism, in which the great tenants *in capite* were each an almost independent potentate over whom the king, his nominal lord, had practically no control.

The justification of the system is the organization for national defence which it provides at a time when nations and lands were only safe in the possession of the strong man armed. For agricultural purposes there was no advantage except comparative security of tenure : the reason of the system was not so much the efficient, as the safe, tilling of land.

It cannot be truly said that feudalism was imposed on England at one time or by one measure. Its greatest effects were seen among those who owned the land ; the condition of the cultivators was at first but little changed. The *Folc-land*

of before the Conquest became the *Terra Regis* of the Norman
kings; the large estates of the principal English nobles were
confiscated by William and distributed by feudal tenure among
his leading followers, who in their turn rewarded with grants
of land to be held of them by military service the armed men
in their train. But it is not probable that the cultivating
portion of the nation was much affected in tenure by the
Conquest, except in those counties whose *fyrd* fought for
Harold at Hastings, or which King William laid waste in the
north, or in the case of the smaller freemen whose land was
too insignificant to confiscate, and whose very insignificance
led them to commend themselves and their land to a lord[1].

According to many writers, the period of the Conquest
was marked by the rapid conversion of independent village
communities into manors dependent on a lord, but Mr
Seebohm's investigations have gone far to disprove this theory,
and if this is so, if communities in form manorial were widely
prevalent before the Conquest, the tenure of land from the
point of view of its cultivators was practically unchanged,
though the tenure of the owners of the land became more
definitely feudal, and the services they rendered more precise.

The English feudal system grows rapidly into completeness:
Ranulf Flambard, the justiciar of William Rufus, is the first
to give it definiteness, by developing its incidents on a logical
basis in the interests of the superior lords. Such legislation
as we find is in the interests of the greater landowners, and
the complaints as to the working of the system are of the
uncertainty of the incidents of its tenure, which enables
tenants to be oppressed by extortionate demands. When the
commutation of personal service for money payments, which
dates from the institution of scutage by Henry II. in 1159,
sets in, the system becomes rather a financial boon to the
lords than a system of national defence, and from the region of
finance we shall be brought to consider the commercial aspect of
the land question.

Of the Saxon tenures of land *Folc-land*, as we have seen,
became the *Terra Regis;* the land of free communities, if any

[1] *v. supra*, pp. 9, 26.

such existed, was probably converted in manorial form into the property of a lord, the tenure of its cultivators changing for the worse, though their dependence ensured their protection. The land of manorial communities was not affected as regards its cultivators, though its lord held by a definite feudal tenure. Heir-land, as a tenure, and so far as large proprietors were concerned, was probably entirely superseded by the feudal tie, though traces of its incidents remained in the restraints on alienation noticed by Glanvil, probably also among the smaller proprietors who did not hold their lands by military service, and in the free tenants of manors; this survival would be helped by the abolition of wills of land. Book-land, in the sense of a tenure continuing under the Anglo-Saxon "books," entirely disappeared, though the grants of land made by charter were of a similar nature, with the addition of the annual services and rents. Tenures, from the landowner's point of view, were much simplified, as landowners fell into two classes ; those holding of the king or of *mesne* lords by military tenures of various kinds, a class which comprised the great mass of feudal tenants, and those holding by free and peaceful services, the free tenants in socage. From the cultivator's point of view we have still the free tenants of the manor holding by free and certain services, contrasted with the *villani*, and lesser manorial tenants, holding, though often freemen themselves, by servile tenure and uncertain services. The history and incidents of the tenure of the landowners however concern us most here.

I. *Alienation during life.* This might affect two interests in the land, those of the heir of the alienor to whom the lands should otherwise descend, and those of the lord of the alienor to whom the services from the land were due, to whom the lands might escheat, and who might have limited his grant by prescribing a line of descent for the land.

To deal first with the case of a simple estate of inheritance, or a grant in fee by the lord, we find in Glanvil, writing about 1180, restraints in the interests of the heir, of which no traces are found afterwards. These appear to be derived from the incidents of Heir-land, though the statement of them is not very precise. According to Glanvil[1], a landowner may during his life alienate a certain portion of his land (*quaedam pars terrae*) with or without the consent of his heir, and he instances grants *in maritagium* to his daughter, or *in eleemosynam* to the church. He defines this *quaedam pars terrae* a little more precisely as *rationabilis pars terrae*[2]. But this alienation is restrained by the condition that it must not deprive his sons of their share of the inheritance. Thus if he possesses land acquired by inheritance, and also land acquired by purchase (*per questum*), he may alienate the whole of his purchased land, without the consent of his heirs; but in the case of his lands acquired by descent, if he has heirs, he may only alienate the "reasonable part," an alienation which his heirs will be bound to warrant. Of his socage lands he cannot grant to any of his sons during life a share of his hereditary land, larger than would descend to that son on his father's death. If he has only acquired land by purchase, the strict rules as to alienation apply to that also; he has only free power of alienation over his purchased land, when he has inherited land with which to satisfy the claims of his children. These restrictions seem framed in the interests of the heir; a similar distinction between inherited and purchased lands appears in the customs of some manors[3].

This passage in Glanvil receives some confirmation from two passages in that part of the unofficial compilation, known inaccurately as the "Laws of Henry I.," which purports to treat of the "Customs of Wessex," viz.—

"Primo patris feudum primogenitus filius habeat; emptiones vero, vel deinceps acquisitiones suas det cui magis velit. Si bocland habeat quam ei parentes dederint, non mittat eam extra cognacionem suam[4]."

"Et nemo forisfaciat feudum suum legitimis heredibus suis, nisi propter feloniam vel reddicionem spontaneam; et

---

[1] Gl. vii. 1.

[2] The *Mirrour of Justice*, c. 1, § 3, speaks of it as "one fourth," but the *Mirrour* is hardly reliable.

[3] e. g. Brigstock in Northampton-

shire, where lands acquired by descent pass to the youngest son, lands acquired by purchase to the eldest. Hazlitt's *Blount*, p. 38.

[4] L. 70, § 21.

nulli liceat forismittere hereditatem suam de parentela sua datione vel venditione...maxime si parentela contradicat[1].

These extracts point to the relics of Heir-land, limited in descent to the family, and protected from alienation, and to its distinction from land acquired by purchase.

It would seem to follow from the feudal theory of a personal and territorial tie between lord and vassal, protection and property granted for service and fidelity, that the tenant under the grant could not substitute another in his place without the consent of his lord. Such was, we know, the rule of continental feudalism, and it is stated by Sir Martin Wright to have been the law of England[2]. It is all but certain however that this rule did not prevail in England; that alienation by a tenant of the whole of his land, so that his feoffee should hold in his place of the chief lord, could not be prevented by his lord, except in the case of tenants in capite, for whose alienations the king's license became requisite about the year 1236. But while this was so, the tenant could not alienate part of his land to be held directly of the lord, for thereby the lord would be deprived of his right to distrain on the whole seigniory for the whole of the services. The tenant could however alienate part of his land to be held of himself as *mesne* lord until the passing of the statute *Quia Emptores*.

Bracton states the law in accordance with this[3]; he says that in cases where there is no special restriction in the donation, the tenant may alienate to whom he will, for though there may be a *damnum* to the chief lord yet there is no *injuria*, or legal wrong. He denies, "*salva pace et reverentia capitalium dominorum*," that the lord loses his services; for the lord, he says, cannot claim more of right than the *certas*

---

[1] L. 88, § 14.

[2] Wright on Tenures, pp. 154—167.

[3] The chief passage of Bracton on the subject, besides that cited in the text, is,—f. 81—si tenens...se dimiserit ex toto de haereditate sua et alium feoffaverit tenendum de domino capitali, ex quo casu tenens absolvitur ab homagio et extinguitur homagium, velit nolit dominus capitalis, et incipit in persona feoffati. The whole subject has been carefully discussed by the Lords' Committee of the Dignity of a Peer, 1st Report p. 398; see also Coke, II. 66.

consuetudines et certum servitium, which he has agreed should be paid to him, " *et sic tollat quod suum fuerit et vadat*[1]."

The tenant could however alienate parts of his land to hold of himself; or he could alienate parts of his land in socage, whereas he held them by military tenure. All these feoffments, sub-feoffments and changes of tenure rendered the chance of the superior lord's obtaining his due services more precarious, for the under-tenant in his turn might enfeoff another to hold of him; or the tenant, instead of enfeoffing an under-tenant for the whole of his lands, might enfeoff four, six, or a dozen, each for a part of the lands.

This difficulty the greater lords attempted to meet by legislation; and in the second re-issue of Magna Charta by Henry III. in 1217 the following clause appears:

" Nullus liber homo de cetero det amplius alicui vel vendat de terra sua, quam ut de residuo terrae suae possit sufficienter fieri domino feodi servitium ei debitum quod pertinet ad feodum illud[2]." For the breach of this proviso there was no penalty: it seems to have been held that the remedy for an alienation which contravened it was not in the chief lord, who might be injured, or in the *mesne* lord who made the grant, " *quia nemo contra factum suum proprium venire potest,*" but in the heir of the *mesne* lord, who could enter and avoid the grant[3]; and it was hoped that such grants would be restrained by the prospect of their nullity at the will of the grantor's heir. But this penalty was altogether inadequate, as the action of the heir could be averted by his joining in the grant, in which case he and his heirs were bound. The proved inadequacy of this remedy led in 1290 to the enactment of the well-known statute, entitled *Quia Emptores,* which is expressly stated to have been passed *ad instantiam magnatum regni.*

---

[1] f. 45, b, cf. f. 46, b. "Cum donatio facta a domino tenenti suo perfecta sit et libera, pura et non conditionalis nec servilis, ex hoc non fit domino injuria, si tenens ulterius dederit, ex hoc enim provenit injuria si contra modum vel conventionem det...Ex liber-tate donationis sequatur, quod donatorius de re data facere possit quod voluerit, si rem ulterius dederit, domino suo non injuriatur, cum totum habuerit quod ad ipsum pertinuerit."

[2] § 39.

[3] Coke, *Ins.* ii. 66.

Before we consider the effect of this statute we may deal with the alienation of lands held by *tenants in capite* direct from the king. Whether from the importance of the due rendering of services from these lands, or from the royal power, the consent of the king was necessary to the alienation of these lands[1]. It was however disputed whether alienation without such a license worked the forfeiture of such lands, or merely entitled the king to a fine, inasmuch as his consent was usually purchased by a fine. In 1304[2] we find the king claiming that an advowson, which had been appendant to a manor held of the king, but had been severed and held in gross, was forfeited for alienation without license: the counsel for the king urge: "If it were a thing that could be distrained such as land, and were holden in chief of the king and alienated against his will, it would be taken into the king's hands until the purchaser had made satisfaction with the king, and if it were a serjeantry, it would be forfeited": but the case seems to have been decided against the king by the peculiar nature of the subject matter.

The dispute was terminated in 1327 by the passing of a statute[3]:—"Whereas divers people of the realm complain that they are grieved because that lands and tenements, which be holden of the king in chief and aliened without license, have been seized heretofore into the king's hands and holden as forfeit, the king will not hold them as forfeit in such a case, but willeth and granteth from henceforth that of such lands and tenements so aliened there shall be reasonable fine taken in the Chancery by due process."

After the passing of this statute the king's officers, probably in the attempt to increase the royal revenue, began to raise questions as to the validity of alienations made in earlier times, as to which there was no record of the king's license. This question was disposed of in 1360 by a statute which enacted that "concerning alienations of lands and tenements made by people which did hold of King Henry III. or of other kings before him, to hold of themselves, such alienations shall

[1] Coke, II. 65, 66. This probably became necessary in the reign of Henry III. Digby, *R. P.*, 3rd ed. pp. 131, 132.

[2] Y. B. 32 Edw. I., pp. 35—38. Rolls Series.

[3] 1 Edw. III. c. 2, § 12.

stand in their force, saving always to the king his prerogative of the time of his grandfather, his father and his own time[1]." The effect of this was that alienations made before the reign of Edward I. would be safe from fine or forfeiture, though made without the king's license, but that alienations without license since that king's accession must pay fines to the Crown. These fines were in the case of alienation with license one third of the annual value of the land, in the case of alienation without license, one year's value[2].

The celebrated statute, *Quia Emptores*[3], forming the first part of the statute of Westminster the Third, and passed in 1290 by a Parliament in which only the Lords Temporal and Spiritual were present, is, as the Bishop of Chester observes, "one of the few acts of legislation which, being passed with a distinct view to the interests of a class, have been found to work to the advantage of the nation generally[4]." A very modern preamble recites that, "Whereas purchasers of lands and tenements held in feud of magnates and others have in time past most often entered into such feuds to the prejudice of the said magnates, in that the free tenants of the said magnates and others have sold their lands and tenements to such purchasers to be held in feud to them and their heirs of the feoffors and their heirs, and not of the chief lords of those feuds, by which the said chief lords have often lost the escheats marriages and wardships appertaining to such lands and tenements held in feud of them; which seemeth very hard and strained to the said magnates and like unto a plain dis-inherison"; and then proceeds "our lord the king...at the instance of the magnates...enacted that any free man may sell his land or tenement or part of it at his will, but so only that the feoffee should hold such land or tenement, or part of it of the same chief lord, and by the same services and customs, that the feoffor held of and by. And if he shall sell any part of the same lands or tenements to anyone the feoffee shall hold it immediately of the chief lord, and shall be bound immediately

---

[1] 34 Edw. III. c. 15.
[2] Report on the Dignity of a Peer, 1. pp. 398—401.
[3] 18 Edw. I.
[4] Stubbs, *S. C.*, p. 468.

by the services which ought to pertain to such chief lord for that part according to the amount of land or tenement sold ; and so in that case that part of the service to be taken from the hand of the feoffor[1] shall cease to the chief lord, because the feoffee owes (it) to the chief lord, being responsible for that part of the service so owed according to the amount of land or tenement sold."

The effect, in brief, of this statute was that tenants in fee (*per feodum*) could no longer alienate their lands in fee so as to create a subordinate fee holden of themselves, but that such alienations would at once destroy the feoffor's interest in the land and make the feoffee a tenant of the lord by the same tenure and services, as those by which the feoffor had held. The statute stopped the creation of new manors, of new tenures in *frankalmoign*, and also the endless subinfeudation which was taking place ; for an alienation in fee now created no new estate, but only changed the person who held the old one. When military services became commuted for fixed money payments, and with the decrease in the value of money these payments became small in amount, the feudal tenures became more vexatious than profitable, and the Act of 1660 which changed them all into estates in free and common socage, virtually converted them into our modern freehold estates in fee simple.

Such was the law as to alienations *inter vivos* of tenements held in fee, or without any restrictions in the grant[2]. And there is nothing in Glanvil which shows that any restrictions on the grant, analogous to the old restricted books, then existed, though he mentions customary restrictions similar to those of Heir-land[3]. But just as grants had been made before the Conquest with restrictions on alienation, so after the Conquest these restrictions reappeared. Their most important form is the *feudum talliatum* or limited fee, in which the descent was cut down[4] to a limited class of heirs. Bracton gives this in two forms :—

---

[1] I read *per manum feoffatoris ; manum feoffati*, the reading of some versions of the statutes and of Coke, makes nonsense.

[2] But see post, p. 47, for a more difficult point as to such alienations.

[3] Gl. VII. 1.

[4] Fr. *tailler*.

"Do tali tantam terram habendam et tenendam sibi et haeredibus suis, quos de carne sua et uxore sibi desponsata, procreatos habuerit"; and

"Do tali et haeredibus suis, si haeredes habuerit de corpore suo[1]." He also cites other instances of restrictions in the grant; e.g.:—

"ne res detur alicui praeterquam ipsi donatori":

"ne cui detur a donatorio vel haeredibus suis[2]." He also mentions twice a form of restriction: "licet donatorio rem datam dare vel vendere cui voluerit, *exceptis viris religiosis et Judaeis*[3]"; where the first part of the restriction appears connected with the policy which terminated in the statute *De Religiosis*[4]. In case of an alienation contrary to these latter conditions, Bracton says that the donor's only remedy will be "*ex conventione agere ad suum interesse,*" both against his donee, and the possessor of the land, to reclaim it, unless there has been an agreement that, in case of an alienation contrary to the terms of the gift, the donor may re-enter on the land, in which case he may do so against the possessor, as well as against the donee.

Where there is a gift in any way restricted by the donor there are two interests which may be created by the restriction and defeated by alienations contrary to it, the interest of the heirs, and the interest of the lord[5]. It is fully established by the time of Bracton that the heirs obtained no independent interest in the land by their mention in the grant, but had only the possibility of succession to their ancestor; the words *haeredibus suis* in a grant "to A and his heirs," to use modern technicalities, were words of limitation and not of purchase[6]." As against his heirs therefore the tenant could freely alienate, and they would be bound to warrant his grants.

As against the lord the matter is not so clear: his right was that of escheat on failure of heirs, or of heirs of the particular

---

[1] Br. ff. 17, b, 47.

[2] Br. ff. 47, b, 48; cf. Britton II. 5, 3, *par la condicioun que il ne doigne ne aliene.*

[3] ff. 13, 47, b.

[4] *v. sub.* pp. 64, 65.

[5] There are no traces in Glanvil of safeguards in the interest of the lord.

[6] Br. f. 17.

class to which he had limited his grant, and we should naturally expect that while, so long as there were heirs in existence of the class named in the grant, their ancestor's grant would avail against them, it would also avail against the lord so long and no longer, for his right of escheat would vest when all such heirs were extinct, and not till then.

In the case however of estates in fee, or "to A and his heirs," Mr Kenelm Digby and Mr Reeves assert[1] that the failure of A's heirs did not cause his fee to escheat, if he had previously alienated. Mr Joshua Williams holds that at the time of Bracton they did[2]. The most important passage on this point is where after citing a grant: *Do tali et haeredibus suis*, Bracton continues:—"Item augere potest donationem, et facere alios quasi heredes...ut si dicat in donatione, 'habendum tali et haeredibus suis, *vel cui terram illam dare et assignare voluerit*, et ego et haeredes mei warrantizabimus eidem T. et haeredibus suis vel cui illam terram dare voluerit vel assignare et eorum haeredibus, contra omnes gentes.' In quo casu si donatorius terram illam dederit vel assignaverit, si donatorius et haeredes sui defecerint, donator et haeredes sui incipiunt esse loco donatorii et haeredum suorum, et pro haerede donatorii erunt, quoad warrantizandum assignatis et haeredibus eorum, per clausulam contentam in charta primi donatoris quod quidem non esset, nisi mentio fiat de assignatis in prima donatione[3]." Mr Digby gathers from this that the only practical effect of the "assigns clause" was to bind the donor to warrant the title of the assigns of the donee, who had the power of alienation without any special words. If this is so, I do not see the use of the limitation to the donee's assigns, as well as the warranty clause to them[4]. Mr Williams' contention seems to me more correct, and it is supported by a passage of Bracton, which neither writer appears to notice: viz.—"Et per hoc quod dicatur 'tali et haeredibus suis' vult donator quod comprehendantur certae personae ad quas descendere debet res donata post mortem donatorii per modum donationis, et per quod

---

[1] Digby, *R. P.*, 3rd ed., p. 137, note 2; Reeves I. 320.

[2] Williams, *R. P.*, 15th ed., p. 63.

[3] Br. f. 17, 17, b.

[4] Cf. Britton II. 4, 2; f. 91.

perpendi poterit, si tales heredes defecerint, quod per modum tacitum reverti debeat res donata ad donatorem[1]." I think therefore that at the time of Bracton a grant to A and his heirs gave A a power of alienation which could be defeated by the lord on the failure of A's heirs, but not till then.

I think this was also the case in what Bracton calls conditional gifts[2]. His curious grant: "A et haeredibus suis, si haeredes habuerit de corpore suo," acts as a grant in fee simple, conditional on A's having heirs of his body: as soon as he has them, his *liberum tenementum* or freehold estate for life will become a *feodum* or freehold estate in fee simple; he can alienate the fee and his alienation will not be defeated by the failure of heirs of his body. But if the donation be *per modum*, as "Do A tantam terram habendam et tenendam sibi et haeredibus suis quos de carne sua procreatos habuerit," A will have at once a freehold and a fee; he can at once alienate it, at any rate for his own life estate, though both his estate will revert and his alienations be defeated if he either has no heirs of the body, or, having had them, they have failed.

The most accepted text-writers agree[3] in stating that before the statute *De Donis Conditionalibus* the donee of an estate granted to him and the heirs of his body, which they call a "conditional gift," could not aliene till he had heirs who satisfied the description in the grant, but that on their birth he could alienate in fee, and (apparently) that his alienations would not be defeated by the failure of heirs of his body. I think it very doubtful whether this is the law as stated by Bracton. He divides donations into[4]:—

I. *Simplex et pura;* ubi nulla est adjecta conditio nec modus.

II. *Sub modo;* modus enim dat legem donationi...haeredes coarctari poterunt per modum donationis: e.g. to A and the heirs of his body.

---

[1] Br. f. 85; cf. Fleta 197; Britton II. 8, 6.

[2] The substance of the next two pages has appeared in an expanded form in the *Law Quarterly Review*, II. 276—278; while a note of an instance of the above 'curious grant' in the law-courts is given in *L. Q. R.* II. 409.

[3] Digby, *R. P.*, 3rd ed., p.138, note 6; p. 154. Pollock, *Land Laws*, p. 64. Williams, *R. P.*, 15th ed., pp. 59, 64.

[4] ff. 17, 17, b, 18.

III. *Conditionalis;* do tali et haeredibus suis, si haeredes habuerit de corpore procreatos.

The second class is sometimes called a Conditional gift, not as Mr Pollock and Mr Digby seem to put it, because of its condition of the *birth* of an heir of the class named, but because, as Bracton and the preamble to the statute De Donis explain, of the express or implied condition of reversion to the donor on *failure* of issue. In conditional donations (class III.) it is true that A has only an estate for life, until issue are born, and that on their birth he has the fee, but Bracton carefully distinguishes this result from that of a *Donatio sub modo,* thus[1]:— "si dicat 'Do tali et haeredibus suis, *si* haeredes habuerit de corpore suo[2],' statim erit liberum tenementum donatorii, sed nunquam feodum nisi cum tales haeredes habuerit, propter conditionem, quae dependet ex fortuna...Si autem sic dicatur 'Do tali et haeredibus suis, de corpore procreatis[3],' statim erit perfecta donatio, *et feodum donatorio,* licet in fine addatur talis condicio (of reversion on failure of heirs), nihilominus perfecta erit donatio ab initio...sed resolvitur sub tali condicione."

By the end of the 13th century, when the statute *De Donis* was passed, the grant to "A and the heirs of his body" seems to have been treated as a conditional gift, Bracton's distinction having disappeared, though one of the examples cited in Britton is Bracton's conditional gift "to A and his heirs, if he have heirs of his body[4]." Britton also writes of it as clearly established that the birth and subsequent failure of heirs of the body did not affect the descent of an estate thus granted and aliened, for, the condition being satisfied by the birth of heirs of A's body, A had then the fee. I should suppose however that even this grant would escheat on the failure of the heirs general of A, though he had aliened it. But we know from Britton and the statute De Donis that by the end of the century the failure of heirs of the body in a grant to "A and his heirs of the body,"

---

[1] f. 47.
[2] A conditional gift.
[3] *donatio sub modo.*
[4] Brit. II. 5, 5. f. 94, A. D. 1290 :

"so that he will be able to give and alien the land although the issue" (? of his body) fail because the condition is satisfied.

did not then give the lord an escheat if A had aliened before
the failure, whatever it might have done at the time of Bracton.
Through this interpretation of limited and conditional grants
lords lost their escheats and their will as expressed in the grant
was defeated: the influence of the great landowners therefore
procured in 1285 the passing of the statute "*De Donis Conditionalibus*[1]" which creates estates tail in the strict sense, *feuda
talliata*, cut off from the fee, and strictly limited to the line
of descent prescribed in the grant. The statute runs thus:—
"First whereas tenements are often given conditionally; (1) as
when one giveth his land to A and his wife and the heirs of
their bodies, such an express condition[2] being added as that if
the man and woman should die without heirs of their bodies,
the land so given should revert to the donor or his heirs[3]; (2) or
when one giveth a tenement to another in *frankmarriage*, which
gift hath a condition annexed, though it be not expressed in the
deed of gift, *i.e.* that if the man and woman should die without
heirs of their bodies, the tenement so given should revert to the
donor or his heirs; (3) or when one giveth a tenement to a
man and the heirs of his body; it seemeth hard to those who
have made grants of this kind and to their heirs that their will
expressed in their gifts has not been and is not observed. For
in all the above cases after offspring has issued from those to
whom the land was so conditionally given, they have the power
of alienating a tenement so given and of disinheriting their
issue from the tenement, contrary to the will of the donors and
the express form of the grant, and moreover whereas, when
issue fail to a man enfeoffed after this wise, the tenement so
given ought to revert to the donor or his heir under the form
contained in the deed of gift, yet, though the issue, if there
were any, may have died, by the deed and feoffment of those to
whom the tenement was so given on condition, (the lords) are

---

[1] The phrase is taken from Bracton,
who derived it from the Roman Law,
but it is used in a different sense from
Bracton's term, being applied here to
Bracton's *donationes sub modo*.

[2] This was implied (*tacita*) in
Bracton; but seems to have been re-

quired to be expressed now; (*vide* 31
Edw. I. Y. B. p. 384, Rolls ed.) "in a
gift in tail the reversion is not saved,
if it be not expressly saved by charter."

[3] Bracton called this not *donatio
conditionalis*, but *donatio perfecta sub
modo*. (v. *ante*, p. 48.)

shut out from the reversion of these tenements, which is plainly contrary to the form of the gift[1]. *Wherefore the King,...* determined that the will of the donor as plainly expressed in the charter of the gift[2] should be observed, so that those[3] to whom the tenement was thus conditionally given should not have the power of alienating such tenement, so that it should not remain to the issue of the donee after his death, or to the donor or his heir, if the donee had no issue or his issue failed." The levying of fines on such estates tail was expressly prohibited, and the operation of the statute was confined to gifts made after its enactment.

The effect of this statute was to enforce the restrictions on alienation and succession, which the will of the donor sought to impose on the land. The tenant in tail in possession might indeed alienate the land, but on his death, the issue to whom the land descended might defeat the alienation by a writ of "*Formedon*[4] *in the Descender*," the lord might defeat it, on failure of the donee's issue, by a writ of "*Formedon in the reverter.*" The alienee therefore had only what was known as a "*base fee,*" which might be only an estate *pur autre vie*, and this in Bracton's time was not even treated as a *liberum tenementum*.

All these restrictions on alienation, and enforcements of the will of the donor in determining succession were clearly imposed at the instance, and in the interest of the greater landowners.

II. *The power of devise at death,* which before the Conquest had only been fettered by the restraints either of the claims of the family on Heirland, or of the conditions of the "book" in bookland, almost entirely disappeared after the Conquest. It had been introduced by church influence, in opposition to the interests of the family and the lord, in order that deathbed repentances might result in temporal profit to the spiritual adviser, whose ministrations effected them. It was defeated by the

---

[1] As I have said (*ante*, p. 47), I do not think this was so at the time of Bracton, in the case of a grant to A and the heirs of his body.

[2] But restrictions might be proved by parol evidence Y. B. 20 Edw. I. p. 130.

[3] The Courts held that the heirs of the donee were also bound. Reeves II. 200.

[4] i.e. *per formam doni.*

interests of the lords, whose pecuniary profits in feudalism were derived in great measure from the payments which they received on the succession and admission of a new tenant to the feud of his dead ancestor. The necessity, if feudalism were to maintain the national defence, of ensuring that lands should be in the hands of a male fit to bear arms, justified the introduction of a fixed rule of succession with payments to the lord by whose allowance it was carried out for his consent to the succession. The abolition of wills was due to the interest of the lords. They only survived in gavelkind lands and by custom in a few towns.

Bracton indeed in one place[1] suggests that the lord could confer by his grant the power of disposing of lands by will, and that wills made in pursuance of such a grant could be enforced. He supposes a grant: "Do tibi et haeredibus tuis, vel cui dare vel assignare in vita, vel in morte legare volueris," and suggests that if the legatee obtained seisin, he could resist an assize brought by the heir, by setting up the grant, or that if out of seisin he can bring a *breve formatum* or special writ, though he admits that such a proceeding was then *inauditum*, unheard of; proceedings in the ecclesiastical courts would, as he says, be stayed by a writ of prohibition. It does not appear that either of these suggestions was ever acted upon; Bracton indeed in a later passage discusses his own devices and pronounces them useless[2]. "Laicum feodum", he says, "legari non possit, nisi in rebus specialibus sicut burgagiis, et unde si laicum feodum petatur ex causa testamentaria in seculari foro, audiri non debet legatarius"; and he holds that an exception by reason of the form of the grant will not lie by a legatee who has seisin against an heir bringing the Assize Mort D'ancester. The suggestions of one part of his work are thus negatived in another. The denial of testamentary power he in several places bases on the maxim "*solus Deus haeredem facit.*"

Exceptions to this prohibition of devise existed in gavelkind lands where many of the old incidents of socage tenure survived. In Kent it seems that a tenant of such lands might dispose by will of all lands which he had acquired by purchase,

---

[1] Br. f. 18, *b*.   [2] Br. f. 49.

but not of inherited land[1]. This distinction was connected with the family claims on Heirland, and is in accordance with the custom of Wessex recorded in the *Leges Henrici Primi*: " Emptiones vel acquisitiones suas det cui magis velit. Terram autem quam ei parentes dederunt non mittat extra cognationem suam"; and also with the customs of some manors, *e.g.* Brigstock in Northamptonshire[2], where lands acquired by descent pass to the youngest son, lands acquired by purchase to the eldest. Similar restrictions on alienation *inter vivos* are recorded in Glanvil[3]; and a similar custom as to devise existed in the town of Shrewsbury, as to which the Assize found that the custom of Shrewsbury allowed a man to devise purchased, but not inherited lands, the will being proved at the Guildhall[4].

Attempts to extend the power of devise seem as yet unsuccessful. Thus in 1293 it was asserted against an heir claiming *Mort D'Ancestor* that the tenements were devisable and not under the common law, whereupon counsel for the heir press for proof of this : " Will you say that these tenements are in a free borough of our Lord the King, or in ancient Demesne," (these being the boroughs which had usually a custom to devise). The legatee attempts to set up a special grant by the Earl of Lincoln of power to devise, apparently based on Bracton's suggestion, but this the court immediately reject as inoperative[5].

With the exception therefore of the survival of the early freedom of devise in gavelkind lands and in the old boroughs, the power of disposing of lands by will is destroyed by feudalism, as contrary to the interest of the lords. .

III. *Succession at death.* With the practical abolition of the power of testamentary disposition the rules of succession at

---

[1] Elton, *Tenures of Kent*, p. 40.

[2] Hazlitt's *Blount*, p. 38.

[3] *supra*, p. 40.

[4] A. D. 1292, Y. B. 20 Edw. I. p. 266. Rolls Series. In Northampton in 1268, a jury found that A on his death-bed devised certain shops to be applied by his executors for his soul *as by the custom well he might*. In Nottingham the jury find that a man or woman having

tenements in the town may on their death-beds devise give or sell to whom they please. Similar customs prevailed in London, Oxford, Canterbury, Scarborough, and Newcastle-on-Tyne. And much of the land in North Wales was devisable with or without writing. Appendix to 4th Report of Real Property Commissioners, p. 25.

[5] Y. B. 21 Edw. I. p. 70. Rolls Ed.

death become of great moment, and the period between the
Conquest and the end of the thirteenth century covers one of
the most important changes in the law of succession. The
Conquest finds equal division among all the sons of the dead
man, or failing sons, among the daughters, to be the law of
the land where restrictions in books or the customs of manorial
communities do not interfere with it. By the year 1300 primogeniture, or succession to the eldest son alone and, failing sons,
to the daughters equally, has become the common law, the old
equal division surviving in gavelkind lands, as in Kent and
parts of Notts, Borough English or *Jüngsten Recht* holding its
ground in Sussex and the older towns, and a variety of customs
existing in different manors, but all as exceptions to the
"common law" of Primogeniture. There is neither space nor
place here for a lengthened discussion of this change, and indeed
no materials for a complete account of the development appear
to me to exist: one can only suggest the leading stages in the
growth of the law.

The introduction of primogeniture into England may be
ascribed to the grants which the Conqueror made to his leading
followers out of the lands which his English enemies forfeited
to him. The feudal system, as a system of national defence,
would logically involve the concentration of lands upon, and the
tenure of fortified places by, one person with sole authority,
rather than by several owners of equal powers in whose differ-
ences of counsel there would be weakness. The importance of
this motive is seen from two incidents in the law: though on
the failure of sons the daughters succeeded equally, as in the old
law, yet castles or strong places must descend to one daughter
only, who should compensate her sisters for their shares, "*propter
jus gladii, quod dividi non potest*[1]." And secondly in the case of
the death of a feudal tenant leaving a young grandson by his
eldest son who had died before his father, and a mature second
son, there was till after the time of Glanvil much doubt as to
whether the uncle or nephew should succeed; for though the
strict rule of primogeniture recognized the grandson's claim, yet
the reason of primogeniture, the holding of military fiefs by one

[1] Br. f. 76.

capable tenant, would have preferred the grown-up man to the orphan boy.

It is therefore in the great military fiefs that we find the first introduction of primogeniture, though even in these the rule is applied with more regard to convenience than to logic. Thus on the death of the Earl of Arundel in 1094 Robert, his eldest son, succeeded to his Norman title and lands, Hugh, his second son, took the English earldom, and three younger sons "had none[1]". Here again the desire to place lands in capable hands is seen to prevail over strict primogeniture, while the Conqueror's policy of not unduly strengthening his turbulent barons is pursued. But on lower levels the great mass of the land of the country is still divided equally among the sons. The unofficial compilation known as the "Laws of William the Conqueror" has the clause : "Si quis paterfamilias casu aliquo sine testamento obierit, pueri inter si haereditatem paternam aequaliter dividant[2]". But the uncertainty of the reigns of William Rufus and Stephen probably led many socage tenants to adopt the safer plan of transmission of their lands undivided to one tenant, their eldest son. In Glanvil, writing about 1180, we find that in military tenures the eldest son succeeds to all the land *secundum jus regni Angliae*[3]. In socage tenures Glanvil distinguishes between lands anciently divisible, in which the old rule of equal division among the sons survives, with the exception that the eldest son must have the chief messuage, paying his brothers their share of its value; and lands not anciently divisible in which either the eldest or the youngest son succeeds according to the local custom. Thus primogeniture appears in lands not held by military tenure, only on the same level as Borough English, a local custom where the old rule of divisibility does not survive or never applied. It is possible that even this customary primogeniture may be a survival from before the Conquest; it may possibly be connected with Mr Seebohm's theory of the primogenitary descent of the equal yardlands in manors[4]. The clearest example we have of it is the

[1] Kenny on Primogeniture, p. 13.   [3] Gl. vii. 3
Dugdale's *Baronage*, p. 27.   [4] v. *ante*, pp. 16, 17.
[2] § 34. Thorpe Inst. p. 207.

position of those tenants of the Canterbury monasteries called "*liberi sokmanni*," who did *certa servitia*, but had primogenitary succession[1].

When legal organization and civil security were revived under Henry II. the merging of local custom in a national and uniform law, and the rules of evidence applied by the itinerant judges tended to establish the rule of primogeniture as a presumption of evidence, just as the absence of security and organization before Glanvil had led to the same result, as a measure of safety. The tendency of the action of the king's judges, consciously or unconsciously, was, by their rules as to procedure, to increase the number of primogenitary holdings. A case in A.D. 1200 is recorded thus:—

Rutland: Gilebertus de Beivill petit versus Willelmum de Beivill duas virgatas terre cum pertinentiis in Gunetorp que ei contingunt de socagio quod fuit patris eorum in eadem villa. Willelmus defendit quod socagium illud nunquam partitum fuit nec debet patiri et hoc offert defendere, etc. Quia Gilebertus nullam probam produxit consideratum est quod Willelmus eat inde sine die et quietus[2].

Mr Kenny speaks of this as establishing a new presumption of primogeniture, on which Mr Pollock remarks that it is only an application of the ordinary rule that the plaintiff must prove his case; as the younger brother does not prove the lands partible, he fails in his suit. But while this is so, it is also true that, as the elder brother would usually take possession, for under either law he was entitled to a share in the land, it would be usually divisibility and not primogenitary succession that must be strictly proved, and the chances would therefore be in favour of the spread of primogeniture.

Bracton in 1260 shows some though not a great advance on Glanvil. He indeed broadly states the proposition: "Si quis plures haberet filios, jus proprietatis semper descendit ad primogenitum, eo quod ipse inventus est primo in rerum natura[3]," and he recognises the strict doctrine of primogeniture

---

[1] Elton, *Tenures of Kent*, p. 106.   *Laws*, p. 208.   Kenny, p. 20.
[2] Pl. de Term. S. Mich. 2 Joh.   [3] f. 64, b.
Abbrev. Placit. 28, b.   Pollock, *Land*

in the question of Representation, by upholding the claims of
the grandson against the uncle. But in the case of socage
land the question is still whether the inheritance is *antiquitus
divisum*; if it is, primogeniture has no place; if it is not,
in the case of lands held by free socage, primogeniture is
established as the universal rule, [*tunc tota remaneat primo-
genito*], instead of, as in the time of Glanvil, appearing as a
local custom, competing with other customs, such as Borough
English. In the case of *villein socage* the old rule still remains,
consuetudo loci erit observanda, and Borough English and
Primogeniture are again mentioned as competing customs.
The chief messuage, if there is only one, goes to the eldest son,
charged with payments to his brothers of the value of their
shares; but if there are several messuages each child in order
of descent takes one so long as any remain[1]. For where the old
rule is not incompatible with the feudal system of defence it
survives.

In a case decided in 1292[2] in which Piers and John de
Mauteby claimed a partition against their elder brother Robert
of land which he claimed as the eldest son of his father, we
have the whole history of a succession for five generations.
Robert de Mauteby (1) had seven sons of whom three, Walter
(2), Geoffrey, and John shared the land; on Walter's death his
son Robert (3) succeeded, though he had five brothers, his six
uncles agreeing and granting for themselves and their heirs that
the land was not partible, and levying a fine. Robert (3) died
leaving a son Walter (4), who succeeded, being apparently an
only son, and he died leaving Robert (5), the present defendant, and two younger brothers, the present claimants. Further,
Robert de C., who held by Knight's service of the lord R.
de Valence, had enfeoffed Bonde as yearly tenant; Bonde
died leaving three sons, of whom the eldest succeeded, and
on his death, leaving five sons his eldest son again succeeded[3].
Thus Robert (5), the defendant showed absence of partition
for five generations in the tenants, and for three generations

---

[1] f. 76.
[2] 20 and 21 Edw. I. Y. B. Rolls
Series, p. 320.

[3] I confess I do not understand how
Bonde comes into the case; previous
writers have omitted to notice him.

in the descent from Bonde. Against this the claimants alleged:—I. that the tenements were held in socage, to which it was answered that, were it so, it did not follow that they were partible, for in some places, and in this, tenements held by socage as well as other tenements were governed by the common law (of primogeniture). II. That the tenements were partible as of right, which was answered by the history of Bonde's tenure and succession; and III. That the tenements had actually been divided when the three sons of Robert (1) shared them, to which it was answered that this was not a partition in fact because four of the children were left out. Metingham, the judge, says, "It seems to us that by the feoffment made to Bonde by R. de Valence's ancestor the tenements are not transferred from the common law" (of primogeniture by which R. de Valence held) "to a special law" of equal division, "unless you can shew that they have since been departed amongst the entire family:" and as they could not, the claimants failed. Here the action of the family itself seems to have established the primogenitary rule.

A similar case is recorded in 1302 concerning lands in Arundel, which the younger brothers claimed as partible against the elder[1]. The younger brothers alleged a partition of the land on the death of their great-great-grandfather in the reign of Richard, and of their great-grandfather in the reign of John; the elder brother alleged a primogenitary succession on the death of his grandfather, and therefore claimed it on the death of his father: upon this the younger brothers asserted that all tenements held of the fee of Arundel were partible, which the elder denied and issue was joined, but the result is not stated. Here we see the actual change in succession, whether finally successful or not, and the matter is decided by the local custom of the fee of Arundel. The complicated state of tenures is shown by a case in 1307[2], where the judge laid down that tenements held by Knight service might be partible, and only required evidence that they had been once divided, to

---

[1] Sedman v. Sedman. Y. B. 30 and 31 Edw. I. pp. 56—60.

Rolls Series. This ruling would tell against primogeniture.

[2] 33—35 Edw. I. Y. B. p. 514.

hold that they were partible of right, for he said "*le departizon· les fet departables.*"

The author of *Fleta*, writing about 1290 merely repeats Bracton, but Britton about the same time asserts primogeniture without qualification[1]:—"Age is material, because he who is the first born is admissible before the younger son of the same father and mother:" that he does not really overlook socage inheritance appears from other parts of his work, in which he recognises divisible inheritances, though he allots the chief mansion to the eldest son or daughter "*pur la priorité de son age,*" or if there are several messuages, to the children in turn, the eldest having the prerogative of choice. He goes on to say[2]:—"Des terres de auncienes demeynes soit usé solom le auncien usage del lu, dount en acun lu tient hom pur usage que le heritage soit departable entre tous les enfants freres et sœurs[3], et en acun lu que le eynznee fiz avera tres tut" (custom of primogeniture) "et en acun lu qe le pusnee de tour les freres eyt tut." (Borough English.)

Before the year 1300 primogeniture is recognised as the common law of the land, to which other customs were exceptions. The *Statutum Walliae*[4] in 1284, after reciting the Welsh custom "quod hereditas partibilis est inter heredes masculos, et a tempore cujus non extitit memoria partibilis extitit," proceeds "aliter usitatum est in Wallia quam in Anglia," without any reference to the existence of the same custom in all gavelkind lands in England. This primogeniture or succession to the eldest son, and, failing sons, to the daughters equally, being then the rule in England in the year 1300, the exceptions were:—

I. The custom of *Gavelkind*, or succession to all the sons equally, and failing sons, to all the daughters equally. This especially prevailed in Kent, but also in other parts[5].

---

[1] Brit. vi. 2, 3. Nicholls ii. 313.

[2] Brit. iii. 8, 4. Mr Kenny (p. 26) overlooks these passages.

[3] This alleged custom goes far beyond gavelkind, but a similar custom is recorded in at least one manor, Wareham. Hazlitt's *Blount.* p. 355: while a similar custom is recorded in Yorkshire, *Raper and Lonsdale* (1810).

12 East 37.

[4] 12 Edw. I.

[5] It survived in parts of Nottinghamshire till the reign of Henry VIII., when it was abolished there by statute (32 Hen. VIII. c. 29), and in many manors.

· II. The custom of *Borough English*, or the succession of the youngest son. This survived chiefly in Sussex, in which county Mr Corner traces 140 manors with such a custom, as against 136 in all the rest of England[1].

III. The numerous intermediate varieties of custom which we find surviving in various manors.

With regard to *Gavelkind* tenure, which is especially associated with Kent, it appears to be a survival of the allodial tenures and incidents which before the Conquest prevailed all over England. If this be so, the problem is to account for its survival in Kent while in most other parts of the country it disappeared. Mr Kenny attributes this survival to three reasons[2]:

(1) That the *villani* of Kent were in reality more free than the *villani* elsewhere; and that consequently Kent as a county was more free than the rest of England at the time of Domesday Book.

(2) That the church was a great landowner in Kent, holding 108 out of 278 knights' fees in capite, and that clerical rule was less harsh than that of lay lords.

(3) That as Kent lay on the high road to the Continent and Normandy, the good feeling of its inhabitants was more important to the Norman Kings, and consequently the ancient privileges of the English were more likely to be preserved.

This is hardly the place for a critical discussion of this very difficult question, but the first two of these reasons appear to me altogether inadequate. (1) The free character of Kent in the time of Domesday is rested on the returns of population which show:—Population 12,205.

Tenants in chief and under tenants	225
socmanni	44
villani	6,597
bordarii	3,118
cotarii	364
servi	1148
burgenses	671,

---

[1] Corner, *Sussex Arch. Trans.* VI. 164, 175.   [2] Kenny, p. 29.

or in a shorter form *Villani*, 54 per cent. : *Bordarii* and *cotarii*[1], 29 per cent. : *Servi*, 9 per cent.

But with this we may compare the neighbouring county of Sussex, which shows :—*Villani*, 57 per cent. : *Bordarii* &c. 31 per cent. : *Servi*, 4 per cent., or the northern county of Yorkshire, with : *Villani*, 63 per cent. : *Bordarii* &c. 23 per cent : *Servi*, 0. Mr Kenny's answer to this, following Mr Elton, is that the *villanus* in Kent is a different person from the *villanus* elsewhere, a far freer man, a free tenant of a manor. On this point I do not wish to recapitulate Mr Seebohm's arguments, but I do not think there is anything to show that the Kentish *villanus* of Domesday was in any different position from the man of the same name in Sussex or in Yorkshire, a freeman holding of the manor by servile tenure. But if he were, it will hardly be contended that he occupied a better position than the *socmanni* or *liberi homines* of the Danish and East Anglian counties. And if we compare the Kentish percentages, with that of Lincolnshire : *sochmanni*, 45 per cent.: *villani*, 30 per cent.: *bordarii* &c. 16 per cent. : *servi*, 0: or of Suffolk: *sochmanni et liberi homines*, 40 per cent.: *villani*, 14 per cent. : *bordarii* &c. 30 per cent. : *servi*, 4 per cent.: there can be no doubt which was the freer county. Yet Kent has maintained the old institutions, which Danish Lincolnshire has lost.

(2) Again, while Kentish landowners show a decidedly clerical character as compared with other counties in England, it does not follow that the inhabitants received any lighter treatment therefrom. The people of Kent had taken such a part in the battle of Hastings, and their lands had been confiscated to such an extent, that at the time of Domesday there was not a single English tenant *in capite* in Kent[2]. And nearly half the church lands in Kent were held under Odo, Bishop of Bayeux, so that as Mr Freeman very justly observes, "there is nothing to show that Kent was better treated than the rest of England. As it was put under Odo, it was perhaps treated a little worse[3]." The County of Middlesex also, which

---

[1] There appears no warrant for the separation of *bordarii* and *cotarii*, whose tenures only differ on minute

points, if at all.

[2] Freeman, *N. C.* v. 810.

[3] See also *N. C.* iii. 538, note.

contained a large proportion of church lands, has not preserved the old incidents of tenure.

I do not therefore think that the causes assigned by Mr Kenny are sufficient to account for the preservation of the old law in Kent, though I cannot assign any that are. It would however in my opinion be a mistake to suppose that the privileges alleged to attach to gavelkind lands at a later period existed continuously from the time of the Conquest. The proverb that "there were no villeins in Kent" has proverbial inaccuracy in face of the 6597 *villani* of Kent in Domesday. When the custom of devise of lands in Kent was established by the Courts, it was so decided on the authority of the records that lands were devisable in Saxon times, and in the teeth of a mass of evidence and decided cases showing that no such custom existed in Kent after the Conquest. Though the Kentish peculiarities of survival are not therefore all due to continuous maintenance, but in many cases to judicial re-establishment of the ancient custom, the reasons for this peculiar position of Kent are in my opinion still unknown.

II. To succession by *Borough English*, a mark of the old tribal household which still remains in some manors, we have already referred[1]. Sussex is its stronghold. The explanation of its origin which refers it to the supposed *jus primae noctis* of the lord may be dismissed as fabulous, even if its natural consequence were not succession to the second rather than to the youngest son. Mr Corner in his exhaustive paper on the subject[2] is of opinion that it must simply be attributed to the will of the particular lord of the manor; he instances, as examples, that it is found in all the manors of the Earls of Warrenne and Surrey in different parts of the country; and also a charter of Simon de Montfort, who at the request of his burgesses of Leicester and by his mere will changed their customary succession in Borough English to a primogenitary rule. Mr Corner goes further and places the origin of this custom after the Norman Conquest, when he supposes it to have been "imposed by the Norman lords as a peculiar mark of serfdom on their

---

[1] *supra*, pp. 10, 59.　　　[2] *Sussex Archaeologia*, vi. 164.

English vassals[1]," and oddly enough cites in favour of this theory the borough of Nottingham, which was in the reign of Edward I. held under two tenures, so that "all the tenements whereof the ancestor died seised in *Burgh Engloyes* ought to descend to the youngest son, and all the tenements in *Burgh Francoyes* to the eldest son as at Common Law[2]". This theory is directly opposed to the usually accepted explanation, which would make the "English borough" in Nottingham the old town, retaining the old Saxon rules, whilst the "French borough" was the new town which had sprung up since the Conquest and was governed by the common law of primogeniture. Mr Corner's suggestion seems to me to fail to account for the continental evidence, and for the curious local distribution of the custom as noted by Mr Elton and Mr Seebohm; and it is moreover contrary to the English evidence of the tenure as prevalent in manors of *Ancient demesne* which dated from before the Cónquest.

III. Besides these two exceptions to the general law of primogeniture, which prevailed in many manors, we have a number of local and intermediate customs of succession in other manors throughout the country. In some the rule of primogeniture is applied to daughters also, the eldest daughter succeeding on failure of sons[3]; in others it is the rule of Borough English which receives extension and in such a case the youngest daughter succeeds[4], instead of the daughters equally, as in other Borough English manors[5], while sometimes the custom extends to the youngest male kinsman of a particular degree, e.g. the youngest son, or brother, or uncle, failing whom the youngest female of the degree succeeds[6]. In some manors the rule of succession varies according to the nature of the lands, as in Brigstock, where the youngest son succeeds to land acquired by descent, (the older lands of the manor,) while as to lands acquired by purchase, the newer rule of primogeniture prevails[7]. Wareham in Dorsetshire has the curious rule of equal division among all the children[8]: in

[1] p. 173.
[2] 1 Edw. I. p. 12, No. 38. Corner, pp. 165, 173.
[3] Hazlitt's *Blount*, pp. 8, 30, 37, 121, 185.
[4] pp. 14, 258, 350.
[5] p. 17.
[6] Corner, *Sussex Arch.* VL 181.
[7] Hazlitt's *Blount*, p. 39.
[8] *Ib.* p. 355.

Dymock, descent is limited to the heirs of the body of the tenant[1]. In Pollington the daughters do not inherit[2], and a similar rule prevailed on the Scotch Marches, where the necessity of having a male tenant of the lands was obvious[3]. At Tregon in Cornwall the tenant was allowed to demise his land for three lives[4]; which in Bedminster unless the copyholder named his successor the lands escheated to the lord, there being apparently no rule of succession[5]. Each manor had in effect its own peculiar customs of succession depending on local usages and history which cannot now be traced.

Restrictions on alienation of land are also to be found in the prohibitions of alienation for certain purposes, and by or to certain persons. To these we now turn.

Alienations of land to religious foundations were, as we have seen, common before the Conquest, and they increased with the power of the Church[6]. By this means the land of the country was withdrawn from contributing to military service, and the lords of the land alienated lost the escheats wardships liveries etc., which would have accrued from the tenancy of a lay holder but were absent from that of a corporation which neither married nor died, and was never an infant[7]. This mischief was first attacked by a clause in the reissue of Magna Carta in 1217[8]: "Non liceat alicui de cetero dare terram suam alicui domui religiosae ita quod illam resumat tenendam de eadem domo, nec liceat alicui domui religiosae terram alicujus sic accipere quod tradat eam illi a quo eam receperit tenendam. Si quis autem de cetero terram suam alicui domui religiosae sic dederit et super hoc convincatur, donum suum penitus cassetur et terra illa domino suo illius feodi incurratur." This clause was practically repeated in the Provisions of Westminster in 1259, which contain the clause: "Viris religiosis non liceat ingredi feodum alicujus sine licentia capitatis domini, de quo scilicet res ipsa immediate tenetur[9]": and Bracton writing

---

[1] Hazlitt's *Blount*, p. 102.
[2] p. 247.
[3] p. 268.
[4] p. 325.
[5] p. 22.
[6] *ante*, p. 19.

[7] Coke, *Ins.* II. 75.
[8] § 43.
[9] § 14. It is this, which is abstracted or recited in the *Statute de Religiosis*, and not *Magna Carta*, as Coke says.

about the same time speaks of a grant of the power of alienation "*exceptis viris religiosis et Judaeis,*" as common, while Lord Coke says he has seen the same clause in many old deeds.

As these Acts proved ineffectual the great Statute *de Religiosis* was passed in 1279. It recites that "men in religion" have entered upon lands in defiance of the former statutes, by which the services due for national defence are lost and the chief lords lose their escheats, and it enacts "quod nullus religiosus aut alius quicunque terras aut tenementa aliqua emere vel vendere, aut sub colore donationis aut termini vel alterius tituli cujuscunque ab aliquo recipere aut alio quovis modo arte vel ingenio sibi appropriare praesumat, sub forisfactura eorundem, per quod ad manum mortuam terrae et tenementa hujusmodi deveniant quoque modo." In case of alienations contrary to the statute the chief lords may enter and seize the lands; and the statute extends to lay corporations as well as "men in religion." It secures the feudal revenues of the chief lords by limiting ecclesiastical endowments, just as the Statute *Quia Emptores,* six years later, protected them by abolishing subinfeudations.

The Statute *De Religiosis* had been occasioned by evasions of the previous Acts on the part of the Clergy, who took leases of lands for long terms of years, and had "used many other devices." It was framed so widely that it might meet their ingenuity but, as Coke quaintly remarks: "ecclesiastical persons, who in this were to be commended that they have ever had the best learned men in the law that they could get of their counsel, found many ways to creep out of this statute[1]. They discovered that the statute did not prohibit the recovery of lands by legal process, and they therefore brought feigned suits against any landowners who wished to convey lands to them, and "recovered" the land, owing to its owners' collusion, by process of law. This expedient was promptly checked by the Statute of Westminster the Second in 1285[2], which provided that all such claims should be submitted to a jury of the county, and that, if they found the demandant church to have

---

[1] Coke, II. 75.   [2] 13 Edw. I. c. 32.   Coke, II. 428.

no right in its demand, the land should be forfeited to the chief lord. ·

To anticipate the next clerical evasion, religious houses obtained the conveyance of lands to feoffees to uses, to be held to the use of religious houses, till this was declared by a Statute of 1392[1], which expressly applied to lay corporations as well, to be mortmain within the Statute *De Religiosis*.

The original purpose of these statutes is plainly and avowedly the interests of the chief lords; indirectly though hardly intentionally they protect the interests of the nation.

A restraint on alienation, depending on the person of the alienor, is found in the rule that no minor could alienate. The age of majority in socage lands was 15, which in lands held by military tenure was increased to 21; but there were also local customs in various towns. Thus in 1339 a writ of Entry, *dum fuit infra aetatem*, (the proceeding to invalidate alienations made under age) was brought against J. in respect of alienations made by J. C.[2] J.'s counsel alleged that the tenements were in Hereford, where the usages are that when a man is of such an age that he knows how to measure an ell of cloth, or reckon up to twelvepence, he can sell his land, and that J. C. was of such an age; but judgment was given against him because the allegation was not certain. The same custom was pleaded as to alienations at Gloucester, with the same result. Bracton mentions the same custom, "where no certain time is defined," as applying to *filius burgensis*, while the daughter is of age when she knows *quod pertinet ad coffer and keye*, which is put about her 14th or 15th year[3]. The case cited shows how the Central Judicature ensured uniformity in the law by breaking down local customs.

Another restraint on alienation, resting on the person of the alienee, is to be found in the prohibition of gifts from husband to wife during coverture. Such a prohibition did not exist in Saxon times, in which the wife, in the absence of express agreement *ad ostium ecclesiae*, would take half her husband's estate at his death if she had children, one third if she were childless. But these shares might by express stipulation either be restricted,

---

[1] 15 Rich. II. c. 5.

[2] Y. B. 13 Edw. III. p. 236. See

also Y. B. 32 and 33 Edw. I. p. 511.

[3] Br. f. 86 b.

or enlarged to half the property if she were childless, or the whole, if she had children. After the Conquest, in lands of military tenure, this right of succession was limited to a life interest in one-third of the lands which the husband possessed — — at the time of the marriage, a proportion which might by express agreement be either restricted, superseded by personalty, or enlarged to one third of all the lands of which he was seised during coverture. In gavelkind, socage, and copyhold lands, \ the share is still one half, and in Borough English towns and in some manors[1], the whole, of the lands. There are still no restrictions in gifts by husband to wife during coverture; at least Glanvil in 1180 is silent as to any.

In Bracton however we find a change: citing three recent decisions he expressly states that: "hujusmodi donationes non valent," when made in excess of the legal dower[2]. He gives no reason for the change, but his follower *Fleta* is more explicit, and says: "quia prohibetur in lege[3]." There can indeed be very little doubt that for this restriction on alienation the influence of the Roman Law is responsible. Though the Statute of Uses provided a circuitous remedy, the restriction was not even partly removed till the Court of Chancery in 1712 held a gift by the husband to the wife without the intervention of a trustee good in equity[4]; but this is only possible where the husband makes himself a trustee for his wife. An instance of failure to make a valid gift is to be found in a recent case, where Vice-Chancellor Hall said: "It is a monstrous state of the law which prevents effect being given to such a gift[5]."

It only remains to notice briefly the formalities required for alienation. These were based on the assumption that publicity of alienation and notoriety of title were important matters. It was therefore necessary that possession should be actually delivered by the grantor to the grantee, or in technical language that there should be "*livery of seisin.*" This was effected in two ways[6]. In "Livery by deed," some object symbolical of the

---

[1] e.g. *Taunton Dene.*
[2] f. 29.
[3] III. 3, 12 and 15.
[4] *Mitchell* v. *Mitchell*, Bunbury,

Rep. p. 207, note.
[5] *Breton* v. *Woolven* (1881), *L. R.* 17 Ch. D. pp. 416, 419.
[6] Co. Litt. 48, a.

land, "the ring or hasp of the door, branch or twig of a tree," was delivered by the grantor to the grantee on the land in question in accordance with the terms of the deed or grant. The object of this is plain from the rule that one Livery of Seisin sufficed for all the tenements in a particular county, but if the tenements were in different counties, there must be one Livery of Seisin in each county. For one jury of the men of the county would decide the title to all lands in that county, and there must therefore be at least one Livery in each county that a jury might be found in that county who were cognizant of it. In "Livery in Law" the presence of the parties on the land was not necessary, but they must be in sight of it, a proceeding devised to effect the alienation of land of which seisin in fact could not be given owing to its being in the hands of a hostile claimant. These precautions were clearly intended to secure notoriety of title and full evidence of alienations. The same purpose was served in manors by public admissions of new tenants and records of alienations and successions in the manorial Court Rolls, in connexion with which customs of symbolical delivery survive in many manors. The old customary law remained for centuries in the lower tenures of land, which were too insignificant to come into the King's Courts, but preserved their ancient customs in the local court of the manor.

The legislation of Edward I. initiates a new era in the Land Law: the Statute of *Quia Emptores* restrained the creation of new tenures, forbidding any alienations but such as either convey the whole interest of the grantor, leaving him without any interest in the land, or convey only a part of the grantor's estate and leave him with a substantial reversion. It allowed a holder in fee to alienate his land in fee, if he surrendered all interest in the land, or to alienate his land in tail, retaining a reversion for himself, but forbade him to alienate his land in fee, while keeping an interest in the land as mesne lord. The Statute *de Donis* ensured that the will of the grantor as expressed in the grant should be observed, and thus strengthened the power of a landowner over his land after his death. This, which from the point of view of the chief lords was a gain of power to alienate, from that of the tenants was a loss of power, as they held their land fettered by restrictions on alienation and by a line of succession marked out by the grantor and enforced by the Statute. The power of disposing of land by will was lost; and the succession to the sons equally, which had protected the interests of the family, was changed in all military tenures to the succession of the eldest son, which was required directly in the interests of the lords, and indirectly in the interests of the State. This rule of primogeniture, at first as a measure of safety in the absence of an efficient central power, then as a measure of unity imposed by a strong and harmonizing government through its Central and Itinerant Judicature, became the common law of the land, the old law of succession to the family being relegated with other local customs to the rank of local exceptions to the general rule. The interests of the lords with some slight reference to the welfare of the State led to the imposition of restraints on the alienation of land for ecclesiastical purposes, while alienations resulting from the conjugal relation were much limited. For about 150 years most properties are subject to strict entail; alienation by their tenants is forbidden; succession to them is defined by the will of their grantor, whose power in this respect is unlimited. The interests of the chief lords or greater land-owners, the class in power, are the reason and origin of the land legislation of Edward I., the system of national defence which is the ultimate justification of the feudal system having but a remote reference to most of the changes which took place.

CHAPTER IV.

THE EVASION OF THE LAW BY FINES AND RECOVERIES.

THE Statute "*De Donis*" in 1285, from the point of view of landowners, fettered the alienation of the greater part of the lands of the kingdom, since the will of the original donor, as fixed in his grant limiting the succession to the land, was to be strictly observed. No power existed of disposing of the land by will, or of defeating the right of the lord to the reversion of the land, if the heirs to whom the land was limited failed.

It is true that the doctrine of Warranty, derived from the old Teutonic procedure, was used to allow the tenant-in-tail to partially set aside the rights of his heir. For, according to that doctrine, the donor of an estate of land was bound to *warrant* the title, or defend the possession, of his donee ; and this obligation extended to the heirs of the donor. The tenant-in-tail therefore, by alienating in fee simple, could on the strict application of the doctrine of warranty, oblige his heirs in tail to warrant his gift, and could thus deprive them of succession under the grant in tail. This proceeding would not defeat the rights of the original donor or lord to the reversion of the land on failure of the class of heirs to whom it was limited in the original grant; but in itself it would allow the tenant-in-tail considerable freedom of alienation *inter vivos*, so as to defeat the claims of his heirs. This power was limited by a decision in 1310, which laid down that the heir in tail was only bound to warrant his ancestor's grants, if he had from his ancestor Assets, or lands in fee of equal value to those alienated; and that, if he had not Assets, he could defeat his ancestor's alienation by a writ of "Formedon in the Descender[1]." This restriction of the obligation to warrant was apparently a piece of judicial legislation, though it had its precedent in a similar restriction imposed by the Statute of — — Gloucester on alienations made by the tenant by the Curtesy, the Statute providing that his heir was only bound to warrant them, if he had lands of the same value descending from his father[2]. The judges had already allowed such an heir to use a writ of "Formedon in the Descender" to defeat his father's alienations[3], and may have felt justified in extending the statutory provision as to Assets to the case of Entails. But they stretched the doctrine of the Statute of Gloucester further in the interests of the heir; for if one heir of a tenant by the Curtesy received assets, the alienation of his ancestor was held good, and subsequent heirs though receiving no assets were bound by it. But in the case of a fee tail, it was necessary that each heir should receive assets in order that the entail might be barred against him, and if he did not, the writ of Formedon was open to him to defeat the alienation[4].

The heir in tail had therefore a practical security in receiving at any rate lands of the same value as those entailed on him, a protection ensured by his writ of "Formedon in the Descender" and by judicial legislation. The lord had absolute security for his reversion or escheat by a writ of "Formedon in the Reverter."

There remains the case where the form of the gift was "to A. and the heirs of his body, and if they fail, then to B. and the heirs of his body." Such a grant is mentioned by Bracton, who calls it a "donatio per modum pluribus," and instances a father granting successive estates tail to his three sons, with a tacit reversion to himself[5]. Shortly after the Statute de Donis B.'s right became recognized with a definite name as a "remainder," and in 1308 we find a writ of "Formedon in the Remainder" recognized as the definite remedy for alienations infringing the

[1] 4 Edw. II. Reeves, II. 202—204.
[2] 6 Edw. I. (1282). Reeves, II. 56.
[3] Reeves, II. 201.
[4] Reeves, II. 310.
[5] Br. f. 18, b.

right of the remainderman[1]. In the case of heirs taking in remainder the doctrine of warranty was more strictly applied[2].
Thus in the case of a feoffment, "to A. in tail, remainder to B. in
tail, remainder to C. in tail," if A. died without issue, and B., succeeding, aliened with warranty and died leaving issue D., D. would
not be bound by the warranty, unless he had assets; but if D.
died without issue, and C. succeeded, C. would be bound by B.'s
warranty, even if he had no assets. And this was called Col-
lateral Warranty, as distinguished from the warranty with Assets,
known as Lineal Warranty. The Courts also contributed to the
strict enforcement of the Statute by the decision[3] that, though
its terms omitted any mention of the heirs of the donee, they
yet were restrained from alienation as well as the donee himself,
a decision which would have made "the will of the donor as
expressed in the grant" extend its power for all eternity, if some
means of defeating it had not been found. They also defeated
some claims on the estate at common law, as resulting in alienations which would prejudice the issue[3].

The result was that the tenant-in-tail had but slight freedom against the heirs of his body, more against the remainderman, but none against the lord. The owner of land could thus
fetter the disposition of his land without any limits as to time,
and the means by which the tenant could escape from his fetters
were of the scantiest application. The evils of this state of
things have been graphically described by Coke and Blackstone[4].
"Children grew disobedient when they knew they could not be
"set aside ; farmers were ousted of their leases made by tenants-
"in-tail, for if such leases had been valid, then under colour of
"long leases the issue had been virtually disinherited; creditors
"were defrauded of their debts, for if tenant-in-tail could have
"charged his estate with their payment, he could also have
"defeated his issue by mortgaging it for as much as it was worth;
"innumerable latent entails were produced to deprive purchasers
"of the lands they had fairly bought; and treasons were en-
"couraged, as estates tail were not liable to forfeiture longer

[1] Reeves, II. 201.   [4] Coke, *Mildmay's Case*: 6 Rep. 40.
[2] Reeves, II. 341.   Blackstone, II. 116.
[3] Reeves, II. 200. Vide *ante*, p. 51.

"than for the tenant's life. So that they were justly branded "as the source of new contentions and mischiefs unknown to the "common law, and almost universally considered as the common "grievance of the realm[1]."

For these reasons all classes in the community, except the great landowners, who in the uncertainty of civil wars desired the protection of their estates from forfeiture for treason, pressed for alterations in the Statute[2]. "The same was attempted and endeavoured to be remedied at divers Parliaments, and divers Bills were exhibited accordingly, but they were always on one pretence or other rejected. For the Lords and Commons, knowing that their estates tail were not to be forfeited for felony or treason,—as their estates of inheritance were before the Act *de Donis*...and finding that they were not answerable for the debts and incumbrances of their ancestors, nor did the sales alienations and leases of their ancestors bind them for the lands which were entailed to their ancestors, they always rejected such bills[3]."

The remedy for this national evil, maintained by that class of the community having power in legislation for their own interests, came from the Law Courts, and is generally associated with the oddly named *Taltarum's Case*[4], decided by the judges in 1472. The process by which judicial ingenuity evaded in the interests of the community a statute passed in the interests of a class was that of a Common Recovery, or fictitious suit brought by a plaintiff in collusion against the tenant-in-tail who wished to alienate his land. This process had already been used by the clergy to evade the Statutes of Mortmain; and its use for that purpose had been restrained by special Statute[5]. It was now brought into play for other purposes.

It is not very material to discuss whether *Taltarum's Case* was the "leading case" to establish the efficacy of common re-

---

[1] Bl. II. 116.

[2] Reeves, II. 841. Godbolt's *Reports*, p. 303.

[3] *Mildmay's Case.* 6 Co. Rep. 40.

[4] Y. B. 12 Edw. IV. 19. Digby, *R. P.* 3rd. ed. p. 211. Taltarum is not a party to the case, but had been the plaintiff in the common recovery alleged, so his immortality is an usurpation and not of right.

[5] V. *supra*, p. 65.

coveries to bar estates tail, or whether their virtue for that purpose had been earlier recognized[1]. Coke says in *Mildmay's Case* that "about 1472 the judges, on consultation had amongst themselves, resolved that an estate tail might be docked and barred by a Common Recovery"[2], while in *Mary Portington's Case*, he says that this method of barring an Estate Tail was "not newly invented in 1472, but oftentimes affirmed before[3];" citing a number of black-letter authorities and concluding that "these resolutions and opinions of law produced the judgment in 1472, which was not of any new invention, but proved and approved by the resolution of the sages of the law at all times after the Act *De Donis* until 1472. And the judges of the law then perceiving what contention and mischiefs had crept into the quiet of the law by these fettered inheritances, on consideration of the said act and of former expositions thereof by the sages of the law gave judgment that in such case the estate tail should be barred."

Taltarum's Case itself does not expressly decide on the validity of a Common Recovery, for while the plaintiff pleads a common recovery suffered by defendant's ancestor, defendant admits it, and sets up a previous estate tail in his ancestor, which alone, he says, was defeated by the common recovery suffered, and the Court agree with him: but it is assumed by both parties and by the Court itself that the Common Recovery in which T. Taltarum is concerned is effectual in barring *some* estate tail in the ancestor.

The procedure of a Common Recovery was based on the doctrine of Warranty, by which the heirs to an entailed estate were barred by the alienation of their ancestor, if they obtained from him Assets, or lands of equal value to those alienated. This proviso was satisfied if they had a right to lands of equal value, though the right might be valueless. The tenant-in-tail, therefore, who wished to alienate arranged that a fictitious suit should be brought against him for the lands: this he met, not by an assertion of his own title, but by calling upon a person

---

[1] See Pollock, p. 83, note. Reeves, iii. 18, where Mr Reeves and Mr Finlason entirely disagree as to the   effect of *Taltarum's Case*.
[2] 6 Rep. 40.
[3] 10 Rep. 37.

whom he alleged to have granted to him the lands in question to warrant or defend the grant he had made. The alleged grantor appeared and acknowledged that he was bound to warrant, but then disappeared and failed to warrant. Whereupon the fictitious plaintiff had judgment against the tenant-in-tail for the lands which he claimed, and the tenant-in-tail had judgment over against the fictitious grantor who had so basely failed to defend his grant. This judgment over, or right to recover lands of equal value from the defaulter, served as Assets to the heir of the tenant-in-tail, who was therefore barred. And Lord Coke expressly rests his defence of Common Recoveries on this "intended recompense[1]," and lays down, "that the judgment given in such case for the tenant-in-tail to have in value is a bar to the estate tail, *although no recompense be had[2]*." For of course the heirs never did recover lands of the value they had lost: the defaulting warrantor was a man of straw, who had no lands to lose, and was indeed in later times, when the comedy was in full working order, the Crier of the Court of Common Pleas, who passed the Law Terms in failing to warrant for the consideration of fourpence per failure.

It is hardly necessary to set out in detail the technicalities of the Common Recovery, either at the time of *Taltarum's Case*, or as ultimately developed by the needs of conveyancing. The proceedings were based on an elaborate series of fictions, and were complicated and expensive in the highest degree; slight slips in them might prove fatal to the title to the land, and it was impossible to find any satisfactory justification for the numerous stages of the procedure, or reasonable explanation of its existence, other than a historical statement of its origin. The Real Property Commissioners in their first Report[3] speak of "the whole mass of technical law relating to common recoveries," as "a mere excrescence on the main body of our laws;" and claim to have shown both their "inaptitude for the purpose for which they (Common Recoveries) have been applied, and the shifts and contrivances to which ingenuity has been obliged to resort in order to render them subservient to those

[1] *Mildmay's Case*, 6 Rep. 40.   37.
[2] *Mary Portington's Case*, 10 Rep.   [3] pp. 30, 31.

purposes." Previous legal authorities indeed rarely, if ever, even attempted to explain the reason of a Common Recovery, but contented themselves with upholding it. "None ought to be heard," says Coke, "in dispute against the legal pillars of common assurances of lands and inheritances[1]." In a case which he mentions, "Hoord an utter barrister of counsel with the plaintiff" (who was barred by a Common Recovery) "rashly and with great ill will inveighed against common recoveries, not knowing the reason and foundation of them, who was with great gravity and some sharpness reproved by Sir J. Dyer, C. J., who said he was not worthy to be of the profession of the law, who durst speak against Common Recoveries, which were the sinews of assurances of inheritances and founded upon great reason and authority", but, adds Coke, "*non omnis capit hoc verbum.*" In short, the procedure in Common Recoveries, invented to evade a Statute, complicated from time to time with provisions against all manner of technical difficulties, became an elaborate and technical formality, whose parts had survived their uses, whose elaboration was only productive of expense, and whose technicality abounded in deadly traps for any but the most skilled and careful lawyers. It had degenerated from a fiction which at its best was cumbrous to a juggle which had hardly the merits of solemnity.

Whatever may have been the law before *Taltarum's Case*, there is no doubt that, after 1472, the way of evading Estates Tail by Common Recoveries was in constant use; and that in consequence the restraints on alienation, and the limited line of succession, imposed by the Statute *de Donis*, were gone. The class legislation of Parliament was defeated by the national legislation of the judges, at the cost of the introduction into Real Property Law of a fiction which, like Frankenstein's monster, became too powerful for its authors.

Another method whereby the strictness of the Statute *De Donis* was evaded was by the *Levying of fines*. A Fine was the compromise of a suit, whether fictitious or actual, as distinguished from a Common Recovery which was the prosecution of a fictitious suit to judgment. In the time of Glanvil, the suit was genuine: "Contingit autem multototiens loquelas

[1] *Mary Portington's Case*, 10 Rep. 40.

motas in Curia domini regis per amicabilem compositionem
et finalem concordiam terminari......dicitur talis concordia
finalis, eo quod finem imponit negotio adeo ut neuter
litigantium ab ea de cetero poterit recedere[1]." The *Modus*
Levandi fines of 1290 recites that a fine solemnly levied
concludeth or barreth all parties and privies to the fine and
their heirs, and all other persons in the world, being of full
age, out of prison, of whole memory and within the four seas
the day of the fine levied, unless they make their claim of
their action within a year and a day[2]. That these Fines were
then well known as means of transferring lands is shown by
the fact that the Statute *de Donis* contains an express provision
against them: "Et si finis super hujusmodi tenemento
imposterum levetur, ipso jure sit nullus, nec habeant haeredes
hujusmodi aut illi ad quos spectat reversio, licet plenae sint
aetatis, in Anglia, et extra prisonam, necesse apponere
clameum suum."

The barring of all claims by non-claim within a year and
a day was abolished by an Act of 1360[3], which shortly provided
that the plea of non-claim of fines should not be taken for a bar
in time to come. This Statute, "whereby" as Coke says "great
contention arose, and few men were sure of their possessions,"
was repealed by an Act of 1483, practically re-enacted by an Act
of 1489[4]. This last statute has been treated by Hume and others
as a deep device of Henry VII. to obtain free alienation in land
by weakening the force of entails. It is sufficient to point out
that entails had practically been destroyed by the time of the
decision as to common recoveries in 1472, and also that the
Statute of Henry VII. only re-enacts the preceding Statute of
Richard III., which, as the Act of an usurper, might be taken to
require confirmation. And Lord Bacon in his history of the
reign discovers no such design in the Act. The two statutes
together give all, except parties to the fine, five years in which
to claim against it. At the expiration of this period they
were barred by non-claim[5]. But heirs in tail or in remainder

---

[1] Gl. viii. 1, 2, 3.

[2] 18 Edw. I.

[3] 34 Edw. III. c. 16.

[4] 1 Rich. III. c. 7. 4 Hen. VII. c.
24. Blackstone, ii. 354. Coke, ii. 518.

[5] Butler's note to Co. Litt. 121, a.

might have no right to the estate till the death of the levier of the fine, their ancestor, and he might survive the fine by more than five years, thus barring their claim. The Statute therefore expressly provides that persons whose title did not accrue till after the levying of the fine should have five years from the accrual of their title in which to claim. Thus the Statute instead of destroying Estates Tail seems rather intended to preserve them[1]. But subsequent provisions of some technicality left it open to doubt whether a fine levied by a tenant-in-tail did not really bind his own issue, and in 1528 the judges were divided on this point, three holding that the Statute of 1489 was not a bar to the issue and four that it was. An Act of 1540 resolved this doubt by the provision that fines levied with proclamations according to the Statute should immediately bar the heirs in tail of the tenant levying the fine, without any time being allowed during which they might claim with success. In this Act, however, certain exceptions were contained, notably that the Act should not apply to lands the alienation of which was restrained by Parliament or to entailed lands the reversion of which was in the king. These exceptions left open to consideration the effect, by itself, of the Statute of 1489, and in the reign of Charles II. eight judges against three held that by the Statute of 1489 also a fine levied by a tenant-in-tail barred his issue[2].

As the system of Common Recoveries as bars to Estates Tail had been definitely established in 1472, the recognition in 1540 of the efficacy of fines for the same purpose was only of secondary importance. There were however two classes of cases in which the use of a fine instead of a common recovery was advisable. If the tenant-in-tail had also a reversion or remainder in fee, there was no one who need be barred but his privies or heirs, and this could be effected by a fine without the necessity of resorting to a common recovery. Secondly, where a remainderman in tail desired to bar the entail, but the person having the freehold in possession refused to play his part in a common recovery, a fine was the only

---

[1] Barrington, *Ancient Statutes*, 3rd ed. p. 402.

[2] *Murray* dem. *Derby* v. *Eyton and Price*, T. Raym. 260.

method open to the remainderman though it would only bar and bind his own issue.

In the history of the defeat of strict entails, fines, though they developed into a system of great complexity and expense[1], are therefore of secondary importance. Their efficiency as devices for barring entails was unintentionally effected by the Statute of 1489, and intentionally confirmed by the Act of 1540. From that time Fines and Recoveries, both fictitious proceedings countenanced by the judges for the purpose of evading the Statute *de Donis*, grew in complexity, losing in their growth any semblance of reality they had once possessed, till they were swept away in 1833 by the "Act to abolish Fines and Recoveries[2]," which substituted for them a simple deed enrolled. Their only merit was that the judges by their use had been enabled to evade in the interests of the Community a statute passed in the interests of a Class.

[1] The Real Property Commissioners give an instance where the amount payable on levying a fine was £4000.

[2] 3 and 4 Will. IV. c. 74.

CHAPTER V.

As the ingenuity of ecclesiastics and their advisers originated the system of common recoveries, by which ultimately
the strictness of entailed estates was broken down, so the
conception of Uses, by which the prohibition against Wills of
Land was evaded and the secrecy of land-transfer was ensured,
was due to clerical endeavours to evade the laws of mortmain.
If uses had been common or well-known at the passing of the
Statute *De Viris Religiosis*, they would have been alluded to
in some more specific way than "alio quovis modo arte vel
ingenio." The ingenuity however which found that common
recoveries were not prohibited by the Act discovered also that
lands might be conveyed to a third person, or held by the
donor himself, to the *use* of some religious house, or in trust
to pay the proceeds to religious purposes with the result of
obeying the letter and evading the spirit of the Statute. But
just as this use of common recoveries had been prohibited by
the Statute of Westminster the Second, so also the evasion of
the Statute of Mortmain by means of uses was prohibited by
a statute of 1391[1], which recited that "of late by subtile
imagination and by art and engine some religious persons"
had evaded the Statute, whereby "men were possessed by
feoffment or by other manner *to the use*[2] *of religious people* of

[1] 15 Rich. II. c. 5.
[2] This word is *oeps* i.e. ad *opus* et
usum. It first appears in a Statute of
1383, "Si ascun alien occupie ascun
benefice, soit il a son *oeps* propre, ou
al *oeps* d'autri. 7 Rich. II. c. 12.
Digby, 3rd ed. p. 274 note.

lands......to amortise[1] them, whereof the said religious persons
take the profits," and enacted that such lands should only
be so alienated by the license of the king or lords or else
sold "*to some other use*[2]" under pain of forfeiture and that "from _ _
henceforth no such purchase be made so that such religious
and other spiritual persons take thereof the profits." The
Statute contains similar provisions as to lay corporations: "and
whereas others be possessed or hereafter shall purchase *to
their use*, and they thereof take the profits......it shall be done
in like manner as is afore said of people religious."

But though religious alienations by means of uses were thus
restrained, the device had been viewed with favour by the laity,
and several statutes were passed to meet the different methods
in which uses were employed to evade common law liabilities.
Thus in 1376 a statute[3] recites that divers people having
incurred debts "do give their tenements and chattels to their
friends by collusion to have the profits thereof at their will,
and after" take sanctuary, "and there do live a great time till
the creditors are forced to take a small parcel of their debts
and release the remnant," and it is enacted that such gifts if
made by collusion shall not protect the goods and chattels from
the creditors. In the following year (1377)[4] another statute
attacks the practice by which persons unjustly in possession
resist the true owners by making feoffments of their lands to
Lords and great men[5], against whom the true owners dare not _
proceed, and declares that such feoffments made by fraud and
maintenance shall be void, and that the persons disseised shall
bring actions within a year against those who take the profits
of the disseised lands. After the prohibition of uses ecclesiastical, further restraining statutes show that the laity fully
appreciated the advantages of the device. Thus a Statute of
1402 extends the remedies of the Statute of 1377 by allowing

---

[1] i.e. alienate in mortmain.
[2] This has been interpreted as a
legislative sanction of *uses*. I think
it only implies the devotion of the
land to secular purposes, without

necessarily any double interest.
[3] 50 Edw. III. c. 6.
[4] 1 Rich. II. c. 9.
[5] To hold to their (the wrongful
possessor's) use.

S.   6

the person disseised to sue the beneficial owner in his lifetime[1],
and a Statute of 1433 extends this advantage to all writs
grounded upon Novel Disseisin, as well as the Assize of Novel
Disseisin itself[2]. A Statute[3] of 1485 recites that persons claiming under entails are hindered by feoffments made to persons
unknown "to the intent that the demandants should not know
against whom they shall take their actions," and enacts that
the demandant shall have his action against "the Pernors[4] of
the profits of the said lands," and that actions shall "proceed
against the said Pernors as if they were tenants indeed or
feoffees to their use of the freehold of the said lands." A
Statute of 1488 attacks the injury to lords who lost their wardships by feoffments to uses, and provides that if the beneficial
owner dies without any will concerning his lands, the lord shall
have his wardship or relief in spite of the feoffment to uses[5].
And a Statute of 1503 recites that whereas creditors were
defrauded of their executions, lords of their reliefs and heriots,
and lords of villeins of the purchases of their villeins, by reason
that the debtors, tenants and villeins "cause by fine, feoffment,
recovery or otherwise divers persons to be seised of the said
lands, only to their use, they taking the profits of the same," it
provides that in each case the cestui-que-use shall be directly
liable[6]. All these statutes however only gave relief to purchasers and others, who came in by act of the law, but were
defeated by "special covinous attempts of the party[7]".

There remained the case of those who "came in by act of
the party," but were defeated by a prior act of that party in
feoffing to uses. A Statute of 1483 attempted comprehensively
to deal with this question[8]. It recited that "by privy and
unknown feoffments great unsurety...grew among the king's
subjects insomuch that no man that buyeth any lands,...nor
women that have jointures nor dowers in any lands...nor men's

---

[1] 4 Hen. IV. c. 7.
[2] 11 Hen. VI. c. 3.
[3] 1 Hen. VII. c. 1.
[4] i.e. cestuis-que-use.
[5] 4 Hen. VII. c. 17.
[6] 19 Hen. VII. c. 15. Similar
statutes on technical points appear in
1378 (2 Rich. II. c. 3), and 1433 (11
Henry VI. c. 5).
[7] Bacon, Reading on the Statute of
Uses, Works, ed. Spedding, vol. VII.
p. 413.
[8] 1 Rich. III. c. 1.

last wills to be performed...nor leases for terms of years or of
life, nor annuities granted for life be in surety because of the
said privy and unknown feoffments," and enacted that all
feoffments and grants made and all acts done by a competent
cestui-que-use should avail to the grantees against such *cestui-
que-use* and his heirs, and all persons claiming an interest in the
land only to the use of the said *cestui-que-use*. Yet, as Coke
says, " So mischievous and sinister is the invention and con-
trivance of uses that they also over-reached the policy and
provisions of the makers of this Act also...so that danger,
trouble, costs and great vexation remained to the realm by
these covinous and fraudulent uses, notwithstanding the said
statute[1]."

An Act of 1483 of a somewhat personal character is of
interest because, according to Bacon, it is " the precedent upon
which the Statute of Uses was drawn, the very mould whereof
that statute was made[2]." It recites that a number of feoffments
to uses have been made to Richard before he was king[3], and
enacts that where he was one of several feoffees to uses, all his
interest shall vest in his co-feoffees, and that where he is sole
feoffee, "all possession, right, title or interest in him" by reason
of such feoffment to uses shall vest in such person or persons
and their heirs to whose use he is so thereof seised :—a clause
almost exactly similar in purport to the important provision in
the Statute of Uses.

In face of this long series of statutes restraining alienations
to uses, and preventing them from being used for purposes of
fraud, or from injuring the rights of others, it is difficult to
understand Bacon's assertion[4]; "that an Use had ·never any
force at all at the common law, but by statute law"; even
though he admits that "there was never any statute made
directly for the benefit of *cestui-que-use*, but always for the

---

[1] *Chudleigh's case*, 1 Co. Rep.
123, a.
[2] 1 Rich. III. c. 5, *Reading*, p. 417.
[3] The King could not be feoffee to
uses, having for this purpose no
Conscience, and therefore, in company

with corporations and aliens, being
incapable of being affected by the
Chancellor. Blackstone, II. 332. Digby,
3rd ed. p. 283.
[4] *Reading*, p. 411.

benefit of strangers and other persons against *cestui-que-use* and
his feoffees, for though by the Statute of Richard III., he might
alter his feoffee, yet that was not the scope of the statute, but
to make good his assurances to other persons, and the other came
in *ex obliquo.*" It is true, as we shall see, that a use had no
recognition or remedy from the common law, but in the face
of these statutes, it is impossible to say that a Use had any
force from Acts, which are only directed to restraining its
creation and annulling its effects.

In spite however of all these statutes, directed, as we have
seen, to ensuring that the device of uses should not protect the
person enjoying the profits of the land from the common law
liabilities attaching to the legal ownership of the land, the
amount of land held subject to uses rapidly increased. Lord
Bacon attributes the first practice of uses to the reign of
Richard II: "and the great multiplying and overspreading of
them was partly during the wars in France," (of the Lancastrian
kings) "which drew most of the nobility to be absent from
their possessions, and partly during the time of the trouble and
civil wars between the two houses about the title of the
crown[1]". For the judges held in the reign of Edward IV., that
a use of lands was not forfeited by attainder[2], so that in the
hazards and vicissitudes of civil wars, a system of land tenure
by uses which protected the land from the misfortunes of an
owner who had identified himself with one side, was even
preferable to the system of estates tail, which preserved the
land to his children, though it allowed his own interest to be
forfeited.

It is evidence of the rapid spread of the conception of uses
that the judges interpreted a Statute of 1414 requiring jurors
to be worth forty shillings in land, to apply to those who had
the use of lands to that amount, who were therefore liable to
serve as jurors; for, as Coke says, "the greater part of the lands
of England in those troublesome and dangerous times was in
use." The position however of *cestui-que-use* had its disadvantages; the feoffee to uses was the legal owner of the land,

[1] *Reading*, p. 411.   was met by private acts of parliament
[2] Spence, Chancery, I. 441.   This   to forfeit such lands.

and if he asserted his legal rights, and refused to recognize the claims on his conscience of the *cestui-que-use*, the remedy of the latter was not clear. The clerical courts would naturally deal with cases of conscience and breaches of faith, but they would be restrained by writ of prohibition from dealing with matters affecting land. The Chancellor does not appear to have given any remedy till the reign of Henry V., and then only a tentative one : we find in 1402[1], the Commons complaining that many grantees and feoffees in trust alienated and charged the tenements granted to them, for which there was no remedy, and praying that one might be provided by Parliament. When recourse to Parliament proved fruitless, the Chancellor's jurisdiction supplied a remedy by enforcing on the conscience of the feoffee to uses, a performance of the trust on which he held the land.

The first recorded application to Chancery is in the reign of Henry V. and is as follows[2]:

"To my worthy and gracious Lord Bishop of Winchester, Chancellor of England. Beseeching meekly your poor bedesman William Dodd, charioteer, who passed over the sea in service with our liege lord and was one of his charioteers in his voyages ; and of his trust feoffed in my land, John Browning and John of Chigwell[3], with my wife, which John and John afterwards against my will and witting put my land to farm, and delivered my movable goods of the value of 20 marks where them list, and thus they keep my deed and the indenture[4], with my movable goods unto mine undoing, unless I have your excellent and gracious help and lordship; beseeching you at reverence of that worthy Prince his soul your father, whose bedeman I am ever, that ye will send for John and John aforesaid, that the cause may be known why they withhold my good[5] to mine undoing ; also which am undone for bruising in service of our liege lord, and in service of that worthy Princess my lady of Clarence, and ever would, if my limbs might, serve worthy prince's son. At reverence of God and of that peerless

---

[1] Spence, I. 443. 4 Hen. IV. Rot. Parl. p. 511.

[2] Cal. Chancery, I. xiii. Digby, 3rd ed. p. 201. I modernise the spelling.

[3] *feoffees to uses.*

[4] ? *creating the use.*

[5] ? does this only refer to the *movable goods* ?

Princess his mother take this matter at heart of alms and charity."

Thenceforward recorded applications become more frequent. Even then there is no sufficient protection to the *cestui-que-use*, for while the feoffee to uses could be bound by conscience and good faith, his heir, who succeeded by a legal title, though he was a privy to the feoffee to uses, was held not answerable to the *subpoena* out of Chancery[1]. So late as the reign of Edward IV. the *cestui-que-use* was driven to the remedy of bill in Parliament. Chancery however, probably in the same reign, remedied this, and even extended the rule, holding that a purchaser for good consideration from the feoffee to uses, with notice of the uses, would be bound by such uses. If he had no notice he held the land free from the uses, but if no valuable consideration passed, notice of the use was presumed and the purchaser was bound[2].

The law therefore was unsatisfactory both to the *cestui-que-use*, and to those having claims on him, and in 1535 an attempt was made to deal with it in a comprehensive way in the celebrated *Statute of Uses*. This Act proceeded on the basis of providing as a general principle, what had hitherto only been asserted in particular instances, that the beneficial owner should stand in the position of and incur all the duties of the legal owner. But there is probably no better statutory illustration of the proposition that, whoever may dispose of the results of a statute, it is certainly not the men who propose it. That the Statute of Uses would result in a comprehensive system of equitable ownership administered by the Chancery, and a complete allowance of wills of land was probably the last thought to occur to its framers. Coke explains their intent to have been "to extirpate and extinguish all uses; for the makers of this Statute," he continues, " having maturely examined the former Statutes and provisions by parliament to reform the great abuses of uses in many particular cases, at last resolved that uses were so subtle and perverse that they could by no policy be governed and reformed," and therefore "they did not

---

[1] Bacon, p. 410.
[2] Bacon, p. 405. Digby, *R. P.* 3rd

ed. p. 282. Y. B. 5 Edw. IV. 7, b.

intend to provide a remedy and reformation by the continua-
tion and preservation, but by the extinction and extirpation
of uses[1]."

The lengthy preamble with which, like most other statutes
of the reign, the Act is provided furnishes the best recital of — -
the results which had followed the introduction of uses, and
which the Statute was intended to prevent. In it is to be
found a complete justification of Coke's statement[2]; "There
were two inventors of uses, fear and fraud; fear in times of
troubles and civil wars, to save their inheritances from being
forfeited, and frauds to defeat due debts, lawful actions, wards,
escheats, mortmains": and also of Bacon's: "that the special
intent unlawful and covinous was the original of uses, though
after it induced to the lawful intents, general and special[3]."
The preamble recites[4] that though the common law has
provided that lands should not be devisable, and should only be
aliened during life by solemn livery and seisin, matter of record,
yet by these fraudulent feoffments and other assurances craftily
made to secret uses intents and trusts, and by wills made on
their death-beds by persons unfit to make them and unduly
influenced by those around them :—(1) many heirs have been
unjustly disinherited: (2) Lords have lost their wardships and
feudal incidents, (for if several persons held as feoffees to uses,
there would never be a minority, or death of the tenant at law,
and the infancy or decease of the *cestui-que-use* would not give
rise to wardship or reliefs): (3) purchasers have no assurance of
their title and no knowledge against whom to claim, (owing to
the secrecy in which uses may be created): (4) husbands lose
their tenancies by the curtesy and wives their dower, because
neither wife nor husband is seised of the lands: (5) the trials
of such secret wills and uses lead to perjury, (for as Bacon says,
"there is a labyrinth of uncertainties and so continual occasion
of false oaths[5]":) (6) the king and lords lose their attainders
and escheats. Wherefore it is enacted that where any person
is seised to the use of another of any estate in land, the *cestui-*

---

[1] *Chudleigh's case*, 1 Co. Rep. 124, a.

[2] *Ibid.* 121, b.

[3] Bacon, p. 411.

[4] 27 Hen. VIII. c. 10.

[5] Works, ed. Spedding, vii 627.

que-use should be deemed to be seised of such estate in land, and that the seisin that was in the feoffee to uses should be transferred to the *cestui-que-use*.

In other words the doctrine of Uses had provided a complicated machinery, by which the person enjoying the benefits of the land was relieved of many of the liabilities attaching to its ownership, while the nature of the "legal owner" was such that that artificial body could evade most of the legal liabilities of the owner. The Statute endeavoured to deal this system its deathblow by providing that the person really enjoying the estate should be treated as the legal owner. Thus a conveyance " to A. to the use of B.," instead of, as before, leaving A. the legal owner, and B. entitled in the Chancery to the profits of the land, converted B., the equitable owner, into the legal owner, leaving A. merely as a "conduit pipe" to pass the property to B. So a grant by A. "to B. to the use of A.," left under the Statute the legal as well as the equitable ownership in A.

The objects of the Statute seem to have been; to prevent the evils resulting from secret transfers of land, which would not arise were its ownership notorious; to practically abolish the system of uses by making them inefficacious; and probably to abolish the system by which wills of land had become possible.

Its results were very different. In the first place legal ingenuity discovered that though the Statute disposed of one use, and prevented it from having its old efficacy, its virtues were exhausted by that operation, and if a second use were created by the grant, the Statute was powerless to touch it. Thus if A. granted lands to B. to the use of C. to the use of D., the Statute made C. the legal owner, but its virtue was then exhausted, because as the metaphysical conception of a use showed, " a use cannot be engendered of a use[1]." C. therefore held as feoffee to uses, D. being the *cestui-que-use*; and as D. had no common law remedy, the Court of Chancery in interfering to protect him, reintroduced the whole doctrine of Uses. Further if the grant ran in the form "to A. upon trust to collect

---

[1] *Tyrrell's Case*, Dyer's Rep. 155, a. Digby, *R. P.* 3rd ed. pp. 326—328, 331.

and pay the rents to B.," A. was evidently intended to be legal owner with an active duty towards B., rather than as in the case of a grant "to A. to allow B. to take the rents," a legal owner subject to a duty of forbearance. Here again the Statute did not apply, and another sphere of action was found for the Court of Chancery. From these two sources, the great doctrine of Trusts was developed.

Again, though the preamble of the Statute recited that lands ought only to be transferred by solemn livery of seisin so as to secure publicity and avoid the evils of secrecy, yet the enacting part of the Statute provided that a conveyance to the use of A. should pass the legal estate and the seisin to A. Now the Court of Chancery had already held that when B. had bargained to sell to A., and A. had paid the price, B., by this Bargain and Sale, held the land to the use of A., and with no other than a bare legal interest in it. But the Statute of Uses carried it further, for when B. held to the use of A., the legal ownership and the seisin passed at once to A., who thus became the legal owner with even less publicity than had been the case before the Statute. This evasion was too glaring to be over-looked, and in the same year, (1535) the *Statute of Enrolments*[1] provided that no estate of inheritance or freehold should pass by any bargain and sale, unless the same should be made in writing and enrolled either in the King's Courts at Westminster, or with the clerk of the peace in the county where the lands were situated. By this means it was hoped that publicity of ownership and transfer would be assured. But the ingenuity of lawyers was as usual too crafty for the precautions of Parliament. The Statute of Enrolments only applied to "estates of inheritance or freehold"; and did not extend to estates less than freehold. If A. therefore bargained and sold or *leased* to B. a term of years, i.e. an interest in the land for a year or years, B. became the legal owner of that estate in the land; if A. then "*released*" to B. the reversion of the land, B.'s two estates would merge, and B. would become tenant in fee simple in possession. Formal and public livery of seisin would be avoided, for B. had as tenant for a term of years a sufficient

[1] 27 Hen. VIII. c. 16.

estate in the land, and thus all securities for publicity were destroyed. This transaction, the lease and release being executed on following days, became the recognized method of conveying freehold lands *inter vivos* till the year 1841, when a statute was passed[1], which simplified the formality by allowing one deed, the release, to take the place of the two, lease and release, which the history of the introduction of the device had rendered necessary. This in its turn was superseded by the "Act to amend the Law of Real Property[2]" in 1845, which, by enacting that all corporeal hereditaments should be deemed to lie in grant as well as in livery, and therefore could be conveyed by a simple deed without any necessity for livery of seisin, removed the necessity for any fiction to supply the place of public livery of seisin, and allowed freehold lands to be conveyed, as incorporeal hereditaments were, by deed.

Thus the framers of the Statute of Uses in their attempt to secure publicity of transfer of land, provided machinery by which secrecy of transfer was ensured. And transfer has, except in certain counties[3], remained secret to this day, though the signs of the times point to a system of registration of title, which will provide publicity of ownership and of alienation, in the interests mainly of cheapness of transfer.

With the way in which the Statute was used in attempting to refetter land by the will of a dead owner by means of springing, shifting, and future uses we shall deal hereafter in considering the history of the rule in restraint of Perpetuities. But we may note that the Statute at once enabled alienations to be made which were impossible under the rules of the old Common Law[4]. Thus a man could, by means of uses, convey a legal estate in land to his wife, a thing impossible under the common law, which forbade alienations between husband and wife *inter vivos*. A man could also under the statute convey lands to himself, as when three old trustees convey land to themselves and a fourth new trustee, by means of a conveyance to A. to the use of the four, a result which could only have been attained by two deeds under the common law.

---

[1] 4 and 5 Vic. c. 21.
[2] 8 and 9 Vic. c. 106 § 2.
[3] e.g. Middlesex and Yorkshire.
[4] Digby, 3rd ed. p. 312.

CHAPTER VI

ANOTHER avowed object of the framers of the Statute of Uses was to abolish the power of devise of lands, which, as the preamble recites, did not exist at the common law, but had been allowed by means of uses, whereby many heirs had unjustly been disinherited. The inroad on the feudal rule which prohibited devise had been effected by means of uses declared in the following manner. The tenant enfeoffed A. into his lands to hold them to his use, until he should declare by deed or parol the uses to which they should be held; he thereafter, usually on his deathbed, declared his will as to those lands, whereupon the feoffees to uses held the lands to the uses declared in his will. By this means a practically complete power of devise was obtained, and was, in numerous reported cases, protected by the Chancellor, acting on the conscience of the feoffee. The technical result is hardly similar to a will, for the tenant is obliged to part with the legal estate in his lands before his death; it is rather akin to settlement, but differs in that the settlor does not declare or limit the settled estate till after the original feoffment, and shortly before his death.

One of the earliest recorded cases is *Rothenhale* v. *Wyching-ham*[1] in the reign of Henry V., where the tenant enfeoffed four persons to have and to hold to them and their heirs for ever, and afterwards by a separate deed "declared his will for the disposition after his death of his lands" that the feoffees "should make full estate" of the lands to his wife for life and by way of remainder to

---

[1] Chan. Cal. II. iii., IV. Digby, 281 n.

his son. The son made a will of his reversionary interest, and
the bill is brought to compel the feoffees to carry it out. Two
similar instances are recorded in the reign of Henry VI. In
one[1], John, Lord Arundel, enfeoffed certain persons in lands "to
the entent that they the said feoffees should performe his will
which he would afterwards declare touching the said manors and
offices." And afterwards by a deed under seal he declared his
will to be that William of Arundel should have an estate tail in
the lands. But on the death of Lord Arundel his son John,
Earl of Arundel entered upon the lands "the said feoffment notwithstanding," and enfeoffed others "to the intent to perform his
will, the which he would afterward declare," and afterwards by a
letter written at Rone[2] directed to his mother, he "declared openly
that it was his will that a state should be made to William of
Arundel in the said lands according to the will of his father in
the most surest wise." But his feoffees to uses refused to so
"make a state," and William of Arundel appeals to the
Chancellor to help him. Another instance[3] records that
Robert Credy, being so sore sick in his bed that for his
sickness he might not be removed, insomuch that in the same
night he died, called to him John and Thomas and said to
them: "Sirs, ye be the men in whom I have great trust before
much other persons, and in especial that such will as I shall
declare to you at this time for my full and last will shall
through your good help by our Lord's mercy be performed": he
then gave and granted to them and their heirs and assigns all
his lands "to this intent that after my death ye shall make
estate," to his wife for life, remainder to his daughter Margaret,
remainder to his right heirs, and he delivers them seisin "to
the intent that this my last will shall be performed by you, as
my trust is that it shall be." They accordingly "make estate to
Alice his wife according to the entent and will afore declared[4]".

That this system of devise became widespread may be

[1] Chan. Cal. i. p. xxxv. Digby, 292.

[2] ? Rouen. The curious informality
of the system is shown here. The will
of the cestui-que-use is alleged by a
letter apparently not under seal, and
not even addressed to the feoffee to
uses, but to a third person.

[3] Cal. Chan. i. xliii. Digby, 293.

[4] I gather that the feoffees to uses
would transfer even their legal estate,
and would not continue to hold it as
trustees.

gathered from its incidental statutory recognition in 1488[1], when a statute against "fraudulent feoffments tending to deprive the king of his wards and liveries," enacts that if any persons are seised in fee to the use of any other person and his heirs, and the *cestui-que-use* dieth "his heir being within age *and no will by him declared nor made in his life touching the premises*"......the lord of the land shall have the same rights of ward and livery, as if the *cestui-que-use* had himself been seised "of that estate so being in use at the time of his death and no such estate" *i.e. by will* "to his use made nor had." Here the system of devise is recognized as an usual occurrence, and as depriving the lord of his wardships.

The informality and insecurity of these wills finds place in the complaints of the Statute of Uses, which recites that hereditaments are conveyed "by Wills and testaments sometimes made by *nude parolx*, sometimes by signs and tokens, and sometimes by writing, and for the most part made by such persons as be visited with sickness, in their extreme agonies, or at such time as they have had scantly any good memory or remembrance: at which times they, being provoked by greedy and covetous persons lying in wait about them, do many times dispose indiscreetly and unadvisedly their lands and inheritances." Though the Statute of Uses does not expressly take away the power of devise, it does so in effect, by destroying any continuing property in the feoffees to uses, who are thereby prevented from remaining seised till the feoffor declares as his will to what uses they are to hold on his death. That this consequence was intended by the framers of the Statute is clear from the clause[2] providing that the wills of persons deceased or who shall die before May 1, 1536, "Shall be good and effectual in the law after such fashion as they were commonly taken at any time within forty years next afore the making of this Act, any thing contained in this Act or in the preamble thereof, or any opinion of the common law to the contrary thereof notwithstanding."

But the power of leaving lands by will was too deeply rooted in popular customs to be torn up by a statute, and the attempt to do so caused great discontent and uncertainty. The will of

---

[1] 4 Hen. VII. c. 17.   [2] 27 Hen. VIII. c. 10 § 9.

Thomas Bourne a tenant in gavel-kind, in 1538, runs: "And whereas there is an Act lately made to avoid uses of wills, yet my mind is that Clement my son shall have my land at Tenderden, and John my son my other lands, and I give my son John forty shillings upon condition that he will abide and stand to the order and dividing of my lands": if he will not, the legacy is to go to testator's wife. In the same year one Sarlys wills that his brother shall have his house at Wy, "if that may be suffered by law;" and John Stace of Leigh wills: "that if the king's last Act in Parliament will not stand with my wife's enjoying the one half of my lands, I will that my executors pay her an annuity of forty shillings[1]."

In the Pilgrimage of Grace, a revolt largely caused by the suppression of the great northern monasteries, one of the merits assigned to monasteries was that they were "the executors of the wills of the people[2]." The demands of the insurgents include[3], "the repeal of the Statute of Uses," and some of the speeches of their leaders show that one great objection to the Statute was that it abolished the power of devise. Sheriff Dymock, the leader of the revolt at Horncastle said[4]: "Masters, there is a statute made whereby all persons be restrained to make their will upon their lands: for now the eldest son must have all his father's lands; and no person to the payment of his debts neither to the advancement of his daughters' marriages can do nothing with their (sic) lands." Aske said of the demand of the insurgents: "They want the Statute of Uses qualified that a man be allowed to bequeath part of his lands by will," and Lord Oxford wrote to Cromwell: "divers things should be reformed and especially the Act of Uses. Younger brothers would none of that in no wise[5]."

Within four years from the enactment of the Statute of Uses it was therefore found necessary to restore by statutory recognition the power of devise, which was accordingly effected by the Statute of Wills, in its full but inaccurate title: "The

[1] 4th Report of Real Property Commissioners. Appendix, p. 29.
[2] Froude, iv. 89—91.
[3] Ibid. iii. 158.

[4] Ibid. iii. 91, note.
[5] Because they were the gainers by wills, elder brothers by intestacy.

Act of Wills, Wards, and Primer Seisin, whereby a man may devise two parts of his land[1]." By this act after a very quaint preamble, which may be not irreverently described as "to the glory of Henry VIII. and God," setting forth that "lawful generations are very great and abundant in the realm," and that the king has "most virtuously considered the mortality that is to every person at God's will and pleasure most common and uncertain," it was enacted that all persons holding lands in fee simple in socage might freely devise of them all by will and testament in writing, or by any act or acts lawfully executed in their life-times[2], and that any person holding lands in knight service might devise two-thirds of them at his pleasure by will in writing. The profits which would result to the king and lords from wardships and primer seisin are carefully preserved to them. From the third part of lands held in knight service, which was not the subject of devise, the lord would obtain his profits of wardship; while, from the fact that the Statute gives security that the lord should have as much land as would give one third of the annual value of the lands, which was the fine payable for leave to alienate land held of the King, it would seem that the proportion of one third was fixed to give security for the fines payable on alienation.

To secure the Crown's rights under this Statute an Act of the same year established the Court of Wards[3]; but the more efficient enforcement of the feudal incidents only rendered them the more unpopular. The confiscation of the land of the monasteries, and its regrant by the King to lay tenants, had placed a larger number of the tenants of the country in the position of holding in chief of the King; and the misfortunes of a tenant *in capite* are feelingly narrated by Blackstone[4] and Sir T. Smith. "The heir on the death of his ancestor, if of full age, was plundered of the first emoluments arising from his inheritance, by way of *relief* and *primer seisin;* and, if under age, of the whole of his estate during infancy. And then......
'when he came to his own, after he was out of *wardship*, his

---

[1] 32 H. VIII. c. 1, explained by 34 and 35 H. VIII. c. 5.

[2] I suppose conveyances in trust.

[3] 32 H. VIII. c. 46.

[4] Com. ii. 76.

woods decayed, houses fallen down, stock wasted and gone, lands let forth and ploughed to be barren,' to reduce him still further, he was yet to pay half a year's profits as a fine for suing out *livery*; and also the price or value of his *marriage*. Add to this the untimely and expensive honour of Knighthood, to make his poverty more completely splendid; and when by these deductions his fortune was so shattered and ruined that perhaps he was obliged to sell his patrimony, he had not even that poor privilege allowed him without paying an exorbitant fine for a license of alienation."

In 1610 an attempt was made to purchase the king's feudal rights for a yearly grant to him, but the transaction, known as the Great Contract, fell through, partly from disagreement as to the price to be paid, partly from other political causes[1]. On February 24, 1645, the Long Parliament passed a resolution assented to by the Lords, that all feudal incidents should be abolished, and all tenures by knight service converted into tenures in free and common socage. This was confirmed by an Act of 1656, and re-enacted in effect in the first year of the Restored Parliament[2].

But while the immediate aim of this series of Acts was the sweeping away of oppressive feudal incidents, whose reason had long been wanting, while their burden had been intensified by the searching zeal of the Court of Wards, its indirect result was to enable all lands held in fee simple to be devised. For, the object of the restriction of devise to only two-thirds of lands held in knight service being swept away with the abolition of that tenure, all lands held in free and common socage could now be freely devised.

The law as to the formalities of devise was still in an unsatisfactory state: for, though the power of disposing of lands by will was open to great frauds unless a clear and well certified declaration of the intention of the testator was obtained, since, the testator being dead, those present at his death could by collusion easily support a feigned parol will or one made inform-

---

[1] Gardner, II. 69, 83, 107. Coke, IV. 202.

[2] 12 Car. II. c. 24. I deal with the circumstances of the passing of this Act in a note hereafter.

ally, without fear of detection, yet the Statute of Wills only required that the will should be in writing : it need not be
signed ; nor need it even be in the testator's own handwriting,
but might be written by another without any sign of attestation
by the testator. This was plainly contrary to good policy, for if
it was desirable that the State should allow a man to arrange
what should happen to his land after his death, and should enforce that arrangement when made, it was still more desirable
that the arrangements which the State enforced should be the
true arrangements which the testator had made. Accordingly
in 1676 the well-known Statute of Frauds provided that all
devises of lands should be in writing, signed by the testator, or
by some other person in his presence and by his express directions, and should be attested and subscribed in the presence of
the testator by three or four credible witnesses, or else be null
and void[1]. Similar provisions were also enacted as to the means
by which a will might be revoked. An Act of 1749 adds
further securities in the same direction, especially in defining
"credible witnesses[2]."

To complete the history, the great Wills Act of 1837[3] simplified and made uniform the law as to the formalities required
for wills of land and personalty with the object of securing that
the will of the testator as to the disposition of his property at
his death should neither be expressed with such laxity as to give
rise to fraud, nor be defeated by the requirement of technicalities which had an ancient history but no modern justification. The "Act to amend the Law of Inheritance[4]" had assisted
this work by reversing some old rules of descent, whose feudal
justification had ceased with the feudal system. Such was the
rule that a will which left to the heir the same estate in lands
as he would have taken without a will was ineffective, the reason
being that under a will the lord would have lost his wardship,
which he might obtain from an heir. The law as to the powers
of disposition of land possessed by a testator has now been put
on a satisfactory footing so far as form is concerned, though the
reasonableness of its substance may be questioned.

[1] 29 Car. II. c. 3, § 5.
[2] 25 Geo. II. c. 6.
[3] 7 Will. IV. and 1 Vic. c. 26, § 9.
[4] 3 and 4 Will. IV. c. 106, § 3.

APPENDIX.

Note on the abolition of Tenures in Chivalry.

As considerable misapprehensions seem to exist as to these proceedings, it may be well to give them somewhat in detail. It is certain that in the reign of James I., a proposal, under the name of "the Great Contract," to commute the feudal rights of the Crown for a yearly revenue payable to the king was considered. This fell through owing partly to extortionate demands on the king's part, and partly to political causes. Coke is certainly wrong in putting the date as 18 Jac. I. (1620), a date which Mr Digby follows: it is probably a slip for 8 Jac. I., (1610), in which year and parliament the Great Contract was discussed[1]. The feudal incidents and the Court of Wards were abolished by resolution of the two Houses in 1645, and in 1656 these resolutions were embodied in an Act[2]. It is also certain that a series of excise taxes were imposed by the Long Parliament and codified by the 19th ordinance in 1656[3]. But there seems to be no connexion in the minds of the legislature between the loss of revenue in 1645 by abolition of the feudal incidents, and the gain of revenue by the excise in 1656. The latter was not intended as a substitute for the former: for though, the land being free, there was a loss of revenue to the State, yet, the expenses of government being less, the need of compensating taxation was not felt.

In the first parliament of Charles II., the matter was at once taken up[4]. On May 3, 1660, it was resolved "That a Committee be appointed to prepare a bill for taking away tenures in chivalry...and to consider and propound to the House how £100,000 may be raised and settled on his Majesty, in compensation for Wardships and Liveries and the Court of Wards." The bill this

---

[1] Gardner, II. 69, 83, 107.　　[3] *Ibid.* 452.
[2] Scobell, 375.　　[4] Commons Journals, VIII. p. 11.

Committee presented was read a first time on May 22[1], a second time, and went into Committee, on May 25[2]: when it was resolved that "The sum of £100,000 to be settled on the King's Majesty his heirs and successors in lieu of taking away (sic) the Court of Wards and Liveries and Tenures *in Capite* and by Knight Service, *be generally charged on all lands*." The bill was then further referred to a Committee. There was a debate on the reported amendments on July 28[3]. On August 4, it was referred to a Committee "to apportion a rate upon the several Counties as equally as they can for the raising of £100,000 per Annum to be settled on his Majesty, in Compensation for Wardships, and Liveries, and the Court of Wards[4]". On November 8, the apportionment of the £100,000 on the respective counties was brought in and the debate adjourned[5]. On November 19 the debate was resumed and adjourned[6]. On November 21, the debate was resumed, when it was moved[7] :"—"That the moiety of the excise of ale[8] &c. shall be settled on the King's Majesty his heirs and successors in full recompense and satisfaction of all Tenures in Capite, and by Knight Service, and of the Courts of Wards and Liveries and in full satisfaction of all Purveyance, [and that the other Moiety of the Revenue of the Excise of Ale &c. be settled upon the King's Majesty during his natural life in further part of the £1,200,000 per annum revenue resolved to be settled on his majesty]." An amendment was moved to leave out the word "moiety[9]," and was negatived. A second amendment was then moved to leave out the words in brackets, and this was carried by a majority of two. The resolution was therefore passed without the second clause, the object of the amendment being apparently not to prejudge the important

[1] VIII. p. 40.
[2] p. 45.
[3] p. 105.
[4] p. 111.
[5] p. 178.
[6] p. 186.
[7] pp. 187, 188.
[8] Bills temporarily continuing the Excise had been passed, July 28, and Aug. 18, 1660: the bill finally imposing

the Excise as part of the royal revenue was passed, Dec. 24, 1660.
[9] The intent of this amendment must either have been by omitting the "first moiety"—to settle the whole excise on the King, as compensation, or by omitting the second moiety, to make the whole excise count as part of the revenue of £1,200,000 to be settled.

question of how the £1,200,000 should be raised, by dealing with it piecemeal.

From this it is clear: (1) that Hallam[1], and Taswell-Langmead following him, are wrong in attributing the majority of two to a division which changed the compensation from a landtax to an excise. This change was affected without a division, the majority of two being on a question relating to the settlement of the ordinary revenue. (2) That any assertions that either the excise, or the abolition of feudal tenures, were new acts of a reactionary Parliament are incorrect; both had a past history; the novelty was their conjunction. Mr Humphreys-Owen's appendix to Mr Brodrick's book[2] seems to me rather to fight the wind. The facts show that a Parliament of Landowners at first agreed that the compensation to the king for his revenues derived only from lands held in chivalry should be *"generally charged on* ALL *lands;"* a proceeding in itself unfair because the lands of all were made to bear the burdens of the few: that, on seeing the amount assessed on each county, this Parliament changed the compensation from a tax on all lands to a tax on ale and spirits, consumed by all people. The land owners in chivalry clearly thus escaped from their own burden, while persons who paid excise found part of it appropriated to defray the debts of others, instead of being used to lessen the taxation necessary for the king's ordinary revenue. Mr Humphreys-Owen in denying that the excise was substituted for the profits of the feudal tenures can hardly have had these facts in his mind.

---

[1] Hallam, *Const. Hist.* II. 424. T.-Langmead, 2nd ed. p. 617.

[2] *English Land and English Landlords.*

CHAPTER VII.

ECONOMICAL CHANGES IN THE LAND-SYSTEM.

BETWEEN the middle of the 14th century and the middle of the 16th, the English system of land cultivation entirely changed; and as the tendency of the changes was undoubtedly to cause larger quantities of land to come into the market, and to make alienations more common, the formed habits of the people naturally led to the repeal or evasion of laws which hindered the free transfer of land.

In the first half of the 14th century the method of cultivation of the land was, on the domain land of the manor by labourers employed by the lord or his bailiff, and paid out of the money commutations which had taken the place of the personal services due from the copyhold tenants; on the copyhold lands of the manor, by copyhold tenants whose holdings were so small that, aided by a common-field system, and common ploughing, they were their own labourers. The land had thus to sustain two classes, a landlord and labourers. The copyhold tenants had their homestead and stock from their lord, and were bound in return to perform personal service in tilling his domain land, a service which by this time had usually been commuted into fixed money payments with which he had hired labourers to cultivate his domain. Alienations of land would usually take place by the hands of the lord, and involving as they frequently did the transfer of a whole manor, would be serious and unusual undertakings. More land probably changed hands through forfeitures and escheats than through direct alienations *inter vivos*.

This system was completely broken up by the effects of the Plague or "Black Death," which devastated England in 1348—49, and again in 1361, and in which nearly half the population perished[1]. The immediate result of this great mortality was a remarkable rise of wages. The Bishop of Chester misunderstands Prof. Thorold Rogers in making him state that it "doubled the rate of wages[2]," as that particular statement only refers to the threshing of corn, and to the years immediately following the plague, while the wages for that labour dropped again in the following years when harvests were plentiful. Prof. Rogers actually states the increases of wages due to the plague thus:—*Reaping Harvest*: general rise of nearly 60 per cent.; *Mowing Grass*: of 34 per cent.; *Thatching*: of 48 per cent.; *Threshing Wheat*: Eastern counties, 32 per cent.; Midland, 40 per cent.; Southern, 33 per cent.; Western, 26 per cent.; Northern, 32 per cent., &c.[3].

He estimates the general effect of the visitation of the Plague, at an average of 50 per cent. rise in wages in all employments[4].

There was great scarcity of labour, and the few labourers who survived demanded high wages. It thus became unprofitable and even impossible for the great lords, who rarely lived on their manors, to hold their lands and cultivate them by bailiffs[5]. They attempted however to continue the old system of tillage by two devices. The famous *Statute of Labourers*[6] endeavoured to fix the rate of wages which the labourers should receive, at the rate at which they had worked before the plague, and to punish them if they would not work for those wages. It recites and confirms an ordinance made, "against the malice of servants, which were idle and not willing to serve after the Pestilence without taking excessive wages," and enacts that they should be bound under pain of imprisonment to serve at the wages of four years before. That this Statute was at any rate not strictly observed is shown by the repeated petitions of the

---

[1] Thorold Rogers, *Hist of Prices*, I. 60.

[2] Stubbs, II. 400, note. Rogers, I. 260.

[3] Rogers, I. 266, 274.

[4] *Ibid.* I. 292.

[5] *Ibid.* I. 24.

[6] 25 Edw. III. c. I.

Commons that it may be enforced.   Prof. Rogers thinks however that in farm labour as distinguished from that of artisans
some effect was produced, as he finds records of the reduction
of the rate of wages in farm accounts of the period[1].   But as a
whole the Statute was inoperative.

The second method resorted to by the landowners was that
of attempting to enforce the personal services of their copyhold
tenants, instead of their payment of the previous pecuniary
commutation.   If this succeeded the labour, being of higher value,
was obtained as practically an increased rent from the villeins.
To the discontent caused by this attempt on the part of the
Lords much of the Peasant Revolt of 1381 is undoubtedly due.

Its failure as an universal expedient led to changes of
cultivation.   For fifty years or so many of the ecclesiastical and
lay corporations let their lands on lease on a system somewhat
similar to the *metayer* system of the South of France, the landlord finding all or a great part of the stock on the farm, the
tenant paying a rent either in money or in kind, and being
bound to return the stock or its value on the expiration of his
lease[2].   But even this extent of participation by the landlord in
the cultivation of the lands passed away and, sooner or later
according to the intelligence and adaptability of the lords, the
land was let out on lease to other cultivators, usually for short
terms, and at first in small lots of 5 or 10 acres[3].   This is so on
corporation lands, which could not be alienated; the lands of
Merton College, Oxford, were all under leases of this description
by the beginning of the 15th century, while New College,
which had retained the system of cultivation under a bailiff till
about 1425, did not arrive at a complete system of leases till
somewhere about 1450[4].   But the lay lords probably alienated
much of their lands in small plots, and the small freeholder, the
forty shillings freeholder of the Act of 1430, became an important factor in England.   The increased number of proprietors
meant an increased amount of transfer and alienation of lands,
and called attention to the restraints on such alienations.

After the Wars of the Roses the commercial element entered

---

[1] Rogers, I. 300.

[2] *Ibid.* I. 24, 25.

[3] Brodrick, *English Land*, p. 18.

[4] Rogers, I. 25.

into the English land-system. The whole baronage had "killed itself out" in the civil wars; the barons who survived found their feudal castles powerless to resist the newly invented gunpowder, and their armed retainers were suppressed by the policy of the Tudors. To them succeeded new men, who had made their wealth in commerce, and whom the growing security of the country tempted to leave the towns and to take up landowning as a business, to be therefore conducted on strict business principles. They saw that the immediate profit to be derived from pasture land was larger than the rent of plough-land, while, as there was no longer need of an armed body of followers, the lord's motive for establishing on his land a number of tenants, who would depend on him and support his cause, was gone. These two motives led to the forced expatriation of the small holders, and the consolidation of their small holdings into large ones. This process is well recounted by Bacon, who says that: "Enclosures at that time began to be more frequent, whereby arable land, which could not be manured without people and families, was turned into pasture, which was easily rid by a few herdsmen; and tenancies for years, lives and at will, whereupon much of the yeomanry lived, were turned into demesnes. This bred a decay of people[1]:" and, as was said in a petition to the Parliament "sheep and cattle drave out Christian labourers." This tendency to consolidate holdings was met by a series of Acts, (which we need only notice in their general effect on the alienation of land), providing, in one Act, that no houses to which 20 acres of land were attached should be destroyed, in another that a suitable dwelling-house should be maintained for every 40 acres of land, with others directed against excessive sheep-farming and enclosures. These Acts, as Bacon continues[1], "did wonderfully concern the might and manner-hood of the kingdom, to have farms as it were of a standard, sufficient to maintain an able body out of penury, and did in effect amortize a great part of the lands of the kingdom unto the hold and occupation of the yeomanry or middle people, of a condition between gentlemen and cottagers or peasants." The

---

[1] Bacon's Works, ed. Spedding, vi. 93, 94, 95.

tendency of these Acts was to ensure the tenure of land by
small farmers or yeomen, who could till their land themselves;
the tendency of the action of the lords was to divorce the tiller
of the soil from any proprietary interest in it, and practically to
create three classes of persons deriving their living from the
land, the landlord, the farmer, and the labourer. So long however as the landowning classes were bent on accumulating land
and founding and maintaining families, it was inevitable that
lawyers should exhaust for them every means of preserving the
land of the family from alienation by any member of the family,
should avail themselves of every device to tie up the land in
strict settlement. The tendency in the three classes has therefore been, for the landlord to accumulate land, for the farm to
become larger, for the labourer to become more dependent, and
to live with less hope of ever acquiring land of his own.

The desire of the landowning classes may have been assisted
by events which, as their immediate result, led to the freer
circulation and transfer of land. The Dissolution of the
Monasteries in 1536 and 1539 confiscated to the Crown lands
estimated at one fifth of the soil of the kingdom, which, being
held by corporations, had never come into the market, but had
been usually cultivated by tenants on favourable leases at low
rents with an option of renewal. These lands were regranted by
the Crown to lay tenants, and thus, in the then state of law and
family custom, rendered alienable, with the result that transfers
of land became far more common. The years following the
Dissolutions contain a large number of Statutes relating to the
tenure and transfer of land; there being ten in the year 1540,
the year of the Statute of Wills, alone; and to this extent
secularizing the lands of the church assisted freedom of alienation. But many of these lands were granted to "new men" of
commercial habits, who yet looked forward to founding families,
and to establishing themselves firmly as members of a landed
nobility. To the aims and desires of these new landowners we
must look for the source of the experiments and attempts in
restraining alienation, which, under the spur of the insecurity
of civil wars, obtained success in the family settlements of
Orlando Bridgman.

Meanwhile the reign of Henry VIII., as compared with that of Edward I., sees a great change in the laws restricting the transfer of land. The landowner's power of restraining his tenant from alienation of the land during his life, and of imposing a particular line of succession on the land on the tenant's death, which had been established by the Statute *De Donis*, is evaded with the help of the judges, by the devices of Fines and Common Recoveries, introduced by the ingenuity of the church, and adopted by lay tenants of land. Through the same channel the Doctrine of Uses is applied to the tenure of lands, with the result of evading the strictness of feudal relations and of the common law to the advantage both of tenant and of lord. Especially by its means was the power of disposing of lands by will given to all landowners, who thus had land free both in their life and at their death. The Statute of Uses aimed at restoring the old common law; at imposing upon the beneficial owner of land the duties and rights attaching to its owner at law; at ensuring publicity of transfer and notoriety of title; and incidentally at checking the secret disposition of lands by will. The irony of fate and the ingenuity of the Courts perverted the Statute from its original purposes. A new system of beneficial ownership, separate from the legal title to land, arose from the ruins which the legislature had made. The means employed to secure publicity of ownership, though supplemented by the Statute of Enrolments, led through the system of Lease and Release to complete secrecy of transfer; and the power of devise, destroyed by the Statute of Uses, was restored four years later, in deference to the strong national feeling in its favour, by the Statute of Wills. Side by side with these legal changes economic transitions were taking place, which furnished the motive power for still further developments in the system of land-tenure. The cultivation of England by lord and peasant gave way to a system of culture by lord, farmer, and labourer: commercial reasons led to large farms, and the desire of new landowners to found a family prompted the accumulation of land in one hand, and the invention of devices to keep on the land the grasp of that hand, though dead. Thus, though from the end of the fifteenth century land is the subject of almost complete freedom of alienation, influences are at work, which after several experiments and failures enable landowners in the seventeenth century to reimpose on the land the fetters of the will of a dead owner, checked only by the rule that those fetters cannot last for a perpetuity. To the history of Family Settlements and of the "Rule against Perpetuities" therefore we now turn.

CHAPTER VIII.

THE 16th and 17th centuries in England were years of almost complete freedom of alienation. Estates Tail, the great device by which landowners had kept lands in their family or under their control, had been broken down by the introduction of Fines and Recoveries, as devices for barring the entail. The absence of the power of devise, which had imposed on the land a line of succession fixed either by the State or the donor, had been at first supplied by the introduction of Uses, and then the incapacity had been deliberately destroyed by the provisions of the Statute of Wills. The tenant could therefore alienate his land freely during his life and devise it at his death to the successor of his choice.

But this freedom of alienation and devise was not congenial to the spirit in which great landowners viewed their land. To preserve their family name and position, to "keep the land in the family" seemed to them a desirable and even laudable object ; to restrain any individual holder of the land from dealing with it so as to interfere with the interest of subsequent generations of the family in the family land was a necessary means to this end. To contrive restraints on alienation and succession which the law would enforce, to ascertain the furthest limits up to which the law would allow the grasp of the dead hand to be kept on the land of the living, was the task set by the great land-owners before their legal advisers. The judges on the other hand endeavoured to protect the interests of the community and of the living tenant, by refusing to recognize many of these attempted restraints, and by bounding those devices which they did allow by a limit beyond which no restraints would be valid, that the land of England might not be tied up in perpetuity.

The endeavour to impose restraints on the land was made along three lines, on one of which it failed completely, while on the other two it achieved considerable success. These three lines were:—

I. Attempts to deprive estates tail of their capacity of suffering fines and recoveries, which failed on all points.

II. Attempts to prevent any particular tenant from having the power to alienate the land, by the device of *Life Estates and Contingent Remainders.*

III. Attempts to attain the same end, and defeat any alienations, if attempted, by the System of *Executory Devises,* founded on Uses and Trusts.

The two latter methods achieved considerable success, and between them account for the present ingenious and fairly effective device of family settlements, which is further supported by the customary law of the landowning class. A definite limit however was imposed on its operation by the rule, to which the Courts gradually gave great precision in dealing with repeated attempts to evade it, which is known as the "*Rule against Perpetuities.*"

I propose briefly to deal with each of these three methods without going too minutely into the technicalities of the law, to explain the limits of the Rule against Perpetuities and to give the history of its growth, concluding this part of the subject with an examination of the present position of the law, and the method in which the system of Family Settlements has been dealt with by Lord Cairns' "Settled Land Act."

I. It was attempted by landowners and their legal advisers to create estates tail, which had as an incident that they could not be barred by a common recovery suffered by the tenant-in-tail[1]. But all these attempts were defeated by the

---

[1] Fearne on Contingent Remainders, p. 257 note. *Taylor* d. *Atkins* v. *Horde,* 1 Burr. 84; *Mildmay's Case,* 6 Rep. 40; *Corbet's Case,* 1 Rep. 83.

judges, who stoutly adhered to a rule, justified rather by policy than by logic, that the power to suffer a common recovery was a privilege, inseparably incident to an estate tail, of which its tenant could not be deprived. Thus in *Corbet's Case*[1] in 1599, the indenture creating the estate tail contained a provision that if the tenant-in-tail or any of his heirs should attempt any alienation by which the estate tail should be barred such estate tail should cease as if he were dead. The judges held such a condition to be void[2], for a condition to be good must defeat the whole of the estate to which it was annexed, whereas this condition did not destroy the estate tail, for the death of the tenant-in-tail would not determine it, but only his death without issue.

This case is believed to have been a fictitious one to obtain the opinion of the Court and pave the way for *Mildmay's Case* in 1605[3], in which a condition in a gift in tail not to suffer a common recovery was held repugnant and against law. In *Sonday's Case*[4] in 1610 an attempt was made to evade common recoveries by leaving land to "A., and if he marry and have issue lawfully begotten then his son to have the land after his decease, if he have no male issue, then B. to have the land ...if any of his sons or their heirs male went about to alien or mortgage the land, then the next heir to enter." But the judges held that this ingenious attempt to make a tenant-in-tail with only a life estate failed, and that A. could at once alienate by recovery, so as to bar the estate tail; for tenant-in-tail could not be restrained from alienating by recovery, either by condition or limitation or devise.

In *Mary Portington's Case*[5] in 1613, the devise in estate tail was made on the condition that if the tenant-in-tail should agree to suffer any recovery, his estate should at once be forfeited, as if he were dead without heirs of his body[6]: but the judges held that no condition or limitation could

---

[1] 1 Rep. 83.

[2] It might be good to restrain discontinuances, though not common recoveries. Co. Litt. 223, b, 224, a.

[3] See note to *Mildmay's Case*, 6 Rep. 40, a.

[4] 9 Rep. 127, a.

[5] 10 Rep. 35, a.

[6] This was contrived to meet the argument in *Corbet's Case*.

restrain a tenant-in-tail from suffering a recovery, nor therefore also from attempting[1] or agreeing to suffer it.

Attempts were also made to take away the power of suffering a common recovery, by obtaining from each tenant-in-tail an agreement in binding form that he would not alien, but these also were held not to bind the tenant-in-tail. Thus in 1608 a case came before Coke[2], in which the donor of an estate tail had made tenant-in-tail enter into a statutory recognizance that he would not alien, "et quia ceux statutes fuerunt en substance de faire un perpetuity, quel le State d'Angleterre ne poit porter, ideo les statutes per le advice de Coke fuerunt cancell." In 1708 a similar attempt was made by means of a covenant against suffering a recovery entered into by the tenant-in-tail in the instrument creating the estate tail, and it was held that the covenant was void[3].

The same end was sought in *Taylor* v. *Shaw*[4], (1664), where it was alleged that by custom, certain copyhold lands held in tail could only be barred by the lord's seizure for forfeiture and not otherwise[5], and the Court held that the law would create a liability to suffer recovery, by the custom of the Court: "if you will allow a customary tail you must allow customary recovery,......otherwise we shall have a fine device of making perpetuities of copyhold estates."

While these attempts were in progress Bacon detected and condemned their object. "There is started up," he said, "a device called perpetuity, which is entail with a conditional proviso tied to his estate not to put away the land from his next heir, and if he do, to forfeit his own estate, which perpetuities, if they stand, would bring in all the former inconveniences subject to entail and far greater." They did not however "stand," for, as Fearne sums up, the power of the tenant-in-tail to suffer a common recovery, or to agree or

[1] *Corbet's Case*, 1 Rep. 83.
[2] Cited Moore, 810.
[3] *Collins* v. *Plummer*, 1 P. Wms. 104.
[4] Carter, 6, 22.
[5] Compare with this the custom in 30 Liber Assisarum, p. 47. Digby, *R.*

P., 3rd ed. p. 227. H. was seised of tenements in Winchester, devisable by custom by will, where there was also a custom that he who is seised by devise cannot make alienation by warranty or otherwise, which shall be a bar to the remainderman or reversioner.

attempt to suffer it, cannot be restrained by condition, limitation, custom, recognizances, statute or covenant. By some of these means however the liberty of a tenant-in-tail to alienate by other methods than a recovery, (as by a feoffment, a fine at common law, or other conveyance working a discontinuance, as opposed to a recovery barring the estate), may be restricted[1]. So also the form of grant in *Mary Portington's Case*, (to the tenant-in-tail, to discontinue on certain conditions as if he had died without issue), which avoids the difficulty raised in *Corbet's Case*, may be applied to impose other conditions on tenant-in-tail, as that his estate shall determine unless he take the arms of the settlor, or that if he succeed to some other estate his estate under that particular deed shall determine. But the chief result of all these attempts was to firmly establish that the tenant of an estate tail could not be restrained from alienating it, so as to bar the entail. In any scheme therefore for preventing alienations tenancies-in-tail could only play a secondary part, for as soon as a tenant-in-tail held the land, liberty of alienation by suffering a common recovery would come in.

To appreciate the methods by which the power of the settlor or testator to restrain the alienation of the land settled or devised was successfully extended, some account of the conception of Remainders is necessary. By the law of England a landowner might at one time and by one grant limit, or carve out of his estate in the land, as many smaller estates, to take effect in succession, as would make up the whole estate he had in the land. Thus having an estate in fee, he might grant his land to A. for life, on A.'s death to B. and the heirs of his body, on failure of the heirs of B.'s body to C. in fee. By this ultimate grant in fee he would exhaust the estate he himself had; A. would have an estate for life in possession, B., an estate tail in remainder, C. an estate in fee in remainder, this "remainder" not being necessarily the whole remaining estate of the donor, but implying that that estate is subsequent to an estate in possession. If the remainder in fee were

[1] Notes to *Corbet's Case*, 1 Rep. 84, a.; Co. Litt. 223, b. ; 224, a.

omitted, part of A.'s estate, an estate in fee, less an estate for
life followed by an estate in tail, would not be disposed of by
his grant, and A. would therefore have an estate in fee in
reversion. Such estates in remainder are of two sorts: *Vested*
and *Contingent.* A Vested Remainder is one which the person
to whom the estate is limited in remainder is ready to take
should the estate previous to his remainder determine at that
moment. A Contingent Remainder is one which the person
designated to take in remainder is not ready to take *eo
instante,* should the preceding estates determine. Thus a grant
to A. for life, remainder to B., a living person, in fee, gives
A. an estate in possession, B. a vested remainder in fee, for,
should A. die, B. is ready to enter on the estate *eo instante.*
But if the grant is to A. for life, remainder to the eldest son
of B. in fee, B. being then unmarried, whether the remainder
will ever take effect is contingent at common law on B.'s
having a son, before A. dies; as soon as that son is born he
becomes entitled to a vested remainder, his estate ceasing to
be contingent on his birth before the death of A. The mark
of a vested as opposed to a contingent remainder is therefore
its present capacity of taking effect in possession, if the prior
estates are determined at once.

The landowner wishing to settle his estate did not obtain
much help from the system of vested remainders. For the
grant of an estate tail to anyone would at once let in a recovery,
which would defeat the estate tail, and give the tenant in tail
full powers to alienate; while a series of life estates, which must
if the remainders were to be vested, be to persons alive at the
date of the settlement or deed, (since such deed or conveyance
passed at once the seisin for all the estates created by it), would
not give any power of settlement beyond the lives of persons in
being.

Contingent remainders afforded a more effective means, for
by giving an estate in tail in remainder to the unborn son of a
living person, the time when effective alienation could take
place was still further postponed.

The law of Contingent Remainders bristles with technicalities
and even absurdities. This is partly owing to the doctrine that

S. 8

livery of seisin conveyed seisin at once to the estate in possession, and to all the particular estates in remainder. But if the estate in remainder were contingent, as where it was to a person then unborn, where, after the grant, was the seisin of that estate? According to the common law it was transferred by the livery, but there was no person in existence to whom it could be transferred; and there must also, it was thought, be something remaining in the original donor to account for his right to the reversion of the land, should the estates preceding the remainder determine before that remainder became vested. To explain this the fictions that the seisin was *in nubibus* or *in gremio legis* were introduced. The doctrine of double possibilities noticed hereafter is also responsible for much of the confusion.

Contingent Remainders were subject to three great rules[1]:—

I. *There must be a particular estate, that is an estate smaller than the grantor's estate, precedent to the estate in remainder.* From this it follows that the space between the grant of a contingent remainder and its taking effect must be filled up with particular estates of freehold, and these particular estates must be valid and continuing; leases at will will not suffice. It further follows that, once a fee simple has been granted, no remainder can be limited upon it; for the fee simple is all that the donor has to grant, and having granted it, he can grant no more. Neither at common law can a fee simple be granted determinable on a particular event, as, " to A. in fee until he marries, and then to B. in fee," for there would be created, not a remainder, but an estate in derogation of a previous estate, which was not allowed at common law. And as the benefit of a condition could only be reserved in favour of the donor and his heirs, a conditional grant could not be used at common law to give an estate to a third party[2].

II. The remainder must commence or pass out of the grantor at the creation of the particular estate.

III. The remainder must vest in the grantee during the continuance of the particular estate, or *eo instante* that it

[1] Blackstone, II. c. 11.   [2] Digby, *R. P.* 3rd ed. p. 223.

determines. From this it results that the determination of the preceding particular estates before the contingent remainder becomes vested destroys such remainder. Further, there must be a possibility that the person to whom the contingent remainder is limited should be in existence at the determination of the preceding particular estate. Thus in a grant "to A. for life, remainder in tail to the eldest son of B," who was then unmarried, there was said to be a possibility that B. would marry and have a son before A. died, and the grant in remainder was therefore good. But in the time of Lord Coke, a grant "to A. for life, remainder to John, the son of B. *or* to the eldest grandson of B," B. being then unmarried, was held void as involving a "double possibility," instead of a single one, for it was possible that B. might have a son, and possible that that son might be called John, two possibilities. It is impossible to defend this rule of "double possibilities" on any grounds of reason: it appears to have arisen from the praiseworthy dislike of the Common law judges to anything savouring of *"perpetuities."* For it is certain that the absence of any such restriction as was in effect contained in the rule against a "possibility on a possibility," whatever the logical merits of the reasoning supporting it, would have favoured the creation of perpetuities of restraints on alienation. And the rule has now been superseded by one form of the "Rule against Perpetuities[1]."

When Contingent Remainders first originated is matter of dispute. Mr Joshua Williams was of opinion that they were not held valid till the reign of Henry VI.[2], and is certain that they were not definitely recognized even then. But there is a grant of the year 1313 to " *R. pro vita, rem diversis filiis suis in generali tallio*," which, if R. had no sons at the time of the grant, would constitute a contingent remainder[3]; while in a case in the *Liber Assisarum* a grant was made "to A. for life so that A. should make no gift or alienation so as to bar the remainder to the *nearer heirs of the blood of the children[4],"*

---

[1] Williams, *R. P.* 15th ed. p. 322, 323. Lord St Leonards in *Cole* v. *Sewell*, 4 Drury and Warren (Ir. Chan.) pp. 1, 32.

[2] *R. P.* 15th ed. p. 312.
[3] 7 Edw. II. Pollock, p. 210.
[4] *propinquioribus haeredibus de sanguine puerorum.*

which, as it was held to refer to the grandchildren of the
donor, would constitute a contingent remainder, if there were
no grandchildren living at the time of the grant[1]. In the discussion of this case two of the counsel put cases of remainders,
which are in fact contingent, being defeated by the failure of
the particular estate preceding them before they became vested,
though in one of the cases, the remainderman is *en ventre de
sa mère* when the particular estate falls in.

Littleton's work shows that in the reign of Edward IV. the
law as to Contingent Remainders was not definitely settled[2].
For, after citing the case of Richel, Chief Justice in the Common Pleas in the reign of Richard II., who granted land to "his
eldest son in tail in condition that if he and his heirs aliened,
their estate should cease, and the land should remain to his
second son in tail on the same condition," Littleton says, "that
all such remainders in the form aforesaid are void and of no
value," and the first reason he gives is: "that in every
remainder which beginneth by a deed, it behoveth that the
remainder be in him to whom the remainder is entailed by force
of the same deed, before the livery of seisin is made to him,
which shall have the freehold." This rule would bar all Contingent Remainders, and was rightly objected to by Coke, who
destroyed it under the guise of exceptions such as when the
remainderman is unborn, and when the remainder depends on
a condition. It is curious also that though Littleton in effect
absolutely condemns Contingent Remainders, one had actually
been allowed as valid by the Courts in the preceeding reign, in
which under a grant to A. for life, remainder to the right heirs
of B., who was then living, on the death of B., and then of A.,
it was held that B.'s heir succeeded, though at the time of the
grant there was no one entitled to the remainder[3].

Mr Williams finds the first examples of settlements with
estates for life, followed by estates tail to children then unborn,
in the reign of Philip and Mary. He finds none previous to

---

[1] Digby, 3rd ed. p. 227.   Society, I. 50.
[2] § 720. Co. Lit. 377, b. Williams,   [3] Juridical Society, I. 51. Will. *R. P.*
On History of Settlements, Juridical   p. 313. Hil. 32. Hen. VI.

the year 1556[1], though he infers that such a mode of limitation had already come into some use; while from the number of settlements merely to husband and wife in special tail, he argues that it could not have been general. *Chudleigh's Case*[2] depends on a similar settlement of a rather complicated nature made in 1556, in which the machinery of feoffment to uses is employed. In this system the vesting of an estate tail, which could be barred by recovery, is postponed by previous estates for life, the first estate tail being limited to a son then unborn.

But this system of settlement was not sufficiently rigid, for if the tenant for life made a tortious feoffment, or forfeited his estate for waste, or did any act amounting to a discontinuance before the remainder in tail had vested, the remaindermen were barred. Thus the very extension of security against alienation, which could only be effected by remainders which were contingent, served to defeat itself, the contingency of the remainders being their destruction. In *Chudleigh's Case*[3], the settlement started with a feoffment by Richard Chudleigh to six feoffees to uses, to the use (1) of Richard Chudleigh and the heirs of his body lawfully to be begotten on each of the six wives of the six feoffees to uses[4]: (2) failing this issue, to the use of the feoffees their heirs and assigns during the life of Christopher Chudleigh, (3) remainder to the sons of Christopher successively in tail male.

During the life of Christopher and before he had a son, the feoffees conveyed to him in fee; and after much argument it was decided that the feoffment made by the feoffees destroyed the contingent remainders of Christopher's sons unborn. This case being argued in 1598, in 1602 it was also decided in *Archer's Case*[5], under a conveyance to A. for life, remainders to the next heir male of A., who was then living, that a feoffment by A. before B.'s death defeated the contingent remainder of the heirs of B.

It was thus clearly established that a device which endeav-

[1] Jurid. Soc. I. 47. The case cited by Pollock may be to children then alive.

[2] 1 Co. Rep. 113, b.

[3] 1 Co. Rep. 121, a.

[4] A most ridiculous and unaccountable limitation.

[5] 1 Co. Rep. 66, b.

oured to fetter alienation by means of life estates, followed by contingent remainders in tail, was always liable to be defeated by discontinuances on the part of the tenant for life. And in an ingenious variation in 1554 an anticipation of the device of trustees to preserve contingent remainders was frustrated by the possibility of a merger of estates, which would shut out the contingent remainders[1].

Other attempts which were made and failed were as follows[2]:—

1. A conveyance containing a series of estates for years, as to A. for 99 years if he should so long live, remainder to his sons and their heirs male, each for 99 years if he should so long live. In this case the Court held the devise to A. and the first contingent remainder good, but the remaining limitations void.

2. A series of life estates, limited by deed as to A. for life, to his heir for life, to his heir for life, &c. This was defeated so far as the grandsons or remote heirs' estate was concerned by the rule of double possibilities.

3. A similar devise in a will was construed by the *Cy Pres* rule, as a life estate to A., remainder in tail to his heir. But this construction was limited to cases where the children of the unborn child received estates tail under the will, and is not applied where the children's estate is either for life or in fee. In those cases such estate is simply treated as void[3]. And this rule of *Cy Pres* is not applied to similar limitations in deeds.

4. A devise to A. for life, remainder to his sons successively in tail, with a direction to trustees on the birth of each son, and on the consequent vesting of his remainder in tail, to revoke that estate in tail and to reduce it to an estate for life also failed[5].

Under the spur of civil troubles an effective device against the insecurity of contingent remainders was at length hit on in the time of the Commonwealth, and it is curious that three

---

[1] *Holcroft's Case*, Moore, 486. Cited Pollock, p. 211.

[2] Real Property Commissioners' Third Report, p. 30.

[3] Williams, *R. P.* p. 325. Fearne,

C. R. p. 204, note, and cases there cited.

[5] *Duke of Marlborough's Case*, 1 Eden, 404.

great epochs in the history of the Laws relating to Land, the Statute *De Donis, Taltarum's Case,* and Bridgman's Conveyances, all follow on civil wars and great insecurity in the nation. The device of trustees, whose duty it was to preserve the contingent remainders, is commonly attributed to Sir Orlando Bridgman, Sir Geoffrey Palmer, and "other eminent counsel who betook themselves to conveyancing, in order by such device to secure in family settlements a provision for the future children of an intended marriage, who before were usually left at the mercy of the particular tenant for life ; and when after the Restoration those gentlemen came to fill the first offices of the law, they supported the invention within reasonable and proper bounds, and introduced it into general use." Orlando Bridgman's conveyances were published in 1682 by his clerk, Johnson, who says of his master that during the Commonwealth, he "betook himself to a sedentary kind of life in his chambers and became the great oracle not only of his fellow sufferers but of the whole nation in matters of law, his very enemies not thinking their estates secure without his advice. Then it was that these precedents were framed and advised by him, they being for the most part settlements between persons of the greatest honour in the kingdom." And in them the device of trustees to preserve contingent remainders is frequently though not invariably employed. Thus in a marriage settlement, the property is conveyed to A. for the term of her natural life. and after the determination of that estate[1], to the use of W. S. for and during the term of the natural life of A. "upon trust only for the preserving the contingent uses and estates hereinafter limited and to make entries for the same, if the same shall be needful, but that the said W. S. shall not convert the rents &c. thereof to his own use, and from and immediately after the death of the said A.," to the use of his wife, with estates tail in remainder to the sons to be born of the marriage[2].

By these means the defeat of contingent remainders by the determination of the estate of the tenant for life before his death, as by some discontinuance, was effectually prevented ; and this

---

[1] Which might precede her natural death.

[2] Bridgman's *Conveyances,* p. 85.

expedient is not found before the conveyances of Orlando Bridgman. Even this was rendered unnecessary in 1845 by the Act to amend the Law of Real Property[1], which provided that Contingent Remainders should be capable of taking effect, notwithstanding the determination by forfeiture, surrender or merger of any preceding estate of freehold, in the same as if such determination had not happened. The same Act also increased freedom of alienation by rendering Contingent Remainders and other future interests alienable, provided that no such alienation by itself should defeat an Estate Tail[2]. But from the time of the Commonwealth it had been possible by means of Contingent Remainders to postpone the time when the settled land would become alienable, in a manner and to an extent only limited by the rule against Perpetuities.

Even greater powers to effect settlements of land were given by the machinery of Uses and Executory Devises, though, whenever a future interest could be construed as a remainder, it was so interpreted and thus rendered subject to the stricter rules of the common law[3].

Executory interests, contrary to the rules of limitation at common law, may be created either under the Statute of Uses *inter vivos*, or by Will. Under the Statute a use of lands may be created, to arise, not on the determination of any recognized estate in the land, in which case it would be treated as a remainder, but on the occurrence of some other event. Thus land may be settled by means of uses on A. in fee, until the marriage of B. and C., when B. shall take a life estate with remainders in tail to the children to be born of the marriage. Here a *springing use* is created, to spring into existence, defeating A'.s previous estate, as soon as B. and C. are married; or there may be a *shifting use*, the use of lands may be limited to A., so long as he remains unmarried, or bears the name and arms of the settlor, and it may be directed that if he marries, or ceases to bear the name and arms, the use shall *shift* to B., on similar conditions. Similar estates in land, known as *Executory Devises* may be created by means of uses in wills, and may be

---

[1] 8 and 9 Vic. c. 106, § 8.   [3] Williams, *R. P.* p. 307.
[2] § 6.

defined as "such a limitation of future estate or interest in lands as the law admits in the case of a will, though contrary to the rules of limitations in conveyances at common law[1]."

These devices were more flexible than the system of remainders, and consequently gave greater power of control over the land to its settlor or devisor[2]. For these executory interests, to use a general term, need no "particular estate" of freehold to support them. A man could leave by will an estate in land to vest on the occurrence of some particular event, and make no provision for the ownership of the land till that event should occur, though such a disposition would at common law at once defeat a remainder. But by such a devise the land would pass to the heir until the event happened, when by a *springing use* the settled estate would spring into existence. By this means an estate to take effect at a future time not too distant could be created without risk of defeat.

By these means also a fee simple or other less estate in land could be created to take effect after a grant in fee simple, or, rather so as to arise and defeat a previous estate in fee on the occurrence of a particular contingency[3]. A devise to A. in fee, but if A. should die before the age of 21, then to B. in fee, would be void in a deed, but valid if made by will as an executory devise[4]. Estates for life with remainders may be limited by will after chattel interests in land such as terms of years, as executory interests, though such limitations would be invalid if made by deed. Powers can also thus be given to particular persons to vary the uses to which the land is held, by the declaration of their will in a prescribed form, even though such declaration defeats their existing estates.

By these means great flexibility was given to the powers of disposition which an owner of land possessed, subject to this, that if the interest in land created could be construed as a contingent remainder rather than as an executory interest; that is, if it must wait for its commencement the determination of

---

[1] Fearne, *C. R.* 386.
[2] Blackstone, II. 173.
[3] This power appears not to have existed so late as 1538, see Dyce, f. 33,

a, *Case of Prior of St Bartholomew.*
Sheldon v. *Gardner,* Vaughan, 25J, 271.
[4] Blackstone, II. 174.

a previous estate in the land by its own weakness, it would be treated as a remainder, and subject to the strict rules of the common law.

Like contingent remainders also, executory interests could not be conveyed by deed, though they might be released and were devisable. The Act to amend the Law of Real Property allowed their alienation by deed, provided that no estate tail was thereby defeated.

The device of contingent remainders, protected by trustees created for that purpose, and the more flexible system of executory interests under the Statute of Uses and by will, placed considerable powers of disposition in the hands of an owner of land. On this power the Courts in their desire to "avoid perpetuities," imposed very definite limits. Their policy is summarized by Blackstone in these words : " Courts of justice will not indulge even wills so as to create a perpetuity, which the law abhors, because by perpetuities, or the settlement of an interest which shall go in the succession prescribed without any power of alienation, estates are made incapable of answering those ends of social commerce, and providing for the sudden contingencies of private life for which property was first established[1]."

[1] Bl. II. 174.

CHAPTER IX.

THE RULE AGAINST PERPETUITIES[1].

UNDER the statute *De Donis*, there was, as we have seen, apparently no limit to the power of a landowner to fetter the alienation of his land, until judicial action allowed the tenant-in-tail to defeat the entail by suffering a recovery. And when this restriction had been imposed it was maintained by the judges against all attempts to create estates tail to which common recoveries should be inapplicable. The great dislike of the common law to "*perpetuities*" or to those settlements of land which attempt to restrain in perpetuity its alienation, has led to the establishment on grounds of public policy of clear rules, limiting and restricting the extent to which dispositions of land by a settlor or testator are good and binding. At first vague definitions and denunciations of a monster "*horrendum informe ingens*," called a Perpetuity, are plentiful, but there is little more. A perpetuity is "an estate inalienable though all mankind join in the conveyance[2]." It is where "if all that have interest join yet they cannot bar or pass the estate[3]." But as to the limits or nature of a perpetuity, the common law judges are silent and content themselves with vaguely denouncing it, as "a thing odious in law, and destructive to the commonwealth,

---

[1] For authorities, see Hargreaves' Argument in *Thellusson Case*, 4 Ves. 247; 2 Jurid. Arg. pp. 1—182. Sir E. Sugden's argument in *Cadell* v. *Palmer*, 1 Cl. and Fin. 372, 384. 3rd Report Real Property Commissioners, pp. 27—44. Williams, *R. P.*, 15th ed. pp. 323, 324, 368—374. Pollock,

Land Laws, pp. 210—215. Lewis *On Perpetuities*, pp. 140—162. Marsden *On Perpetuities*. Gray, *Rule against Perpetuities*. Boston. 1886.

[2] *Scattergood* v. *Edge*, (1697) 1 Salk. 229.

[3] *Washburne* v. *Downes*, (1672) 1 Ch. Ca. 213.

which would stop the commerce and prevent the circulation of the property of the kingdom[1]."

Mr Sanders clearly defines a perpetuity in these words: "a perpetuity is a future limitation, restraining the owner of the estate from aliening the fee simple of the property, discharged of such future use or estate, before the event is determined or the period is arrived when such future estate is to arise. If that event or period be within the bounds prescribed by law, it is not a perpetuity[2]." It is now firmly established that no limitation by way of executory interest or devise which will take effect after the expiration of 21 years from the death of any person living at the creation of the limitation is valid[3]. It is also laid down with regard to contingent remainders that no life estate can be given to any unborn person, followed by any estate to the child of such unborn person[4]. It has been argued that this is merely a tentative form of the Rule against Perpetuities in Executory Interests[5], but the better opinion appears to be that the two rules are distinct and separate[6].

During the 16th and the beginning of the 17th centuries there are on the one hand a series of vague denunciations of Perpetuities from the bench, without any clear distinction as to what restraints on alienation were allowable and what void; on the other several cases of some obscurity by which executory devises, contrary to the common law were yet recognized[7]. The first case of any importance however is that of *Pells* v. *Brown*[8] (1621), which Lord Kenyon described as " the foundation and as it were the Magna Charta of our Law," on this subject, but which Mr Hargreaves, though he admits " the almost unreachable subtlity of the reasoning," " does not feel to have furnished much of the code of executory devise[9]." In that case, land was devised to A. in fee, and if he died without issue,

[1] Vernon, 164 (1683).

[2] Sanders, *Uses and Trusts*, 5th ed. p. 204.

[3] *Cadell* v. *Palmer* (1833), 1 Cl. and Fin. 372.

[4] Williams, *R. P.* p. 323.

[5] Lewis *On Perpetuities*, pp. 408, et seq. Pollock, p. 213.

[6] Per Joshua Williams.

[7] Hargreaves, pp. 30—32. Especially *Matthew Manning's Case*, 8 Co. Rep. 94 b.

[8] Cro. Jac. 590.

[9] pp. 33—35.

leaving B. surviving, then to B. in fee. A. suffered a common recovery, and then devised the land to C., and died without issue, leaving B. surviving. B. claimed against C., and it was held (1), that the executory limitation to B. was good ; (2), (Doddrïdge, J. dissentiente) that it could not be barred by a common recovery in the part of A. The case therefore, though it supports the power and efficacy of executory devises, does not impose or define any limits to that power, and in it the contingency did not exceed one life in being.

In *Snow* v. *Cutler* (1660—1670)[1], there was a devise to the heirs of the body of the testator's wife if they should attain the age of fourteen, (a devise which if valid, might have extended to a life in being, and fourteen years after). The devise was objected to as being to a person unborn, and also on Lord Coke's metaphysical doctrine of a double possibility, the birth of a child and that child's living to be fourteen years old. All the judges, following *Pell* v. *Brown*, agreed that an executory devise to take effect within the compass of a life was good, " but not after a death without issue, for that would make a perpetuity," and that an executory devise could not be barred by a common recovery, but on the question whether the particular devise, notwithstanding the double contingency was good, the court were equally divided, and, as Levinz says, " I suppose the parties afterwards agreed, for I heard nothing of it after." Some years previously in *Goring* v. *Bickerstaff*[2] (1664), it ·had been decided in the case of a chattel, that "the limitation of a term to several persons in remainder one after another, if they be all in being and alive together is good, and doth in no sort tend to the perpetuity of a chattel"; for the lives are all wearing out together, "all the candles are lighted at once[3]," and the limitations really amount to the life of a person in being with an added machinery to secure a long life.

In *Taylor* v. *Biddall*[4], (1672), there was a devise to A. until

---

[1] 1 Lev. 135. T. Raym. 162. 1 Keb. 752, 800. 2 Keb. 11, 145, 296. 1 Sid. 153.

[2] Pollexfen, 31. Lewis, *Perp.* pp. 142.

[3] This phrase is attributed by Lord Bridgman to Lord Hale. Hargreaves, 46.

[4] 2 Mod. 289.

her son B. was 21, and then to B. in fee, but if B. should not live
to be 21, then to the heirs of the body of C. in fee. B. died
under 21, while C. was still alive; but it was held that the
devise was good: this certainly appears to allow a devise to
lives in being and 21 years afterwards, yet it hardly seems at
first to have been treated as an authority for that proposition.
For in *Lloyd* v. *Carew* (1697)[1] there was a devise to the heirs
of the body of husband and wife, but if they died without such
heirs, then, if the wife's heir should within a year of the death
of the survivor of them pay to the husband's heir £4000, the
land was to go to the wife's heir in fee. This was in effect a
settlement on two lives in being, and a year beyond; yet it was
held void in the Common Pleas, apparently because the contingency was too remote, though the decree was reversed in the
Lords. And in *Luddington* v. *Kime*[2] (1696), while Powell, J.
would allow a posthumous son to take, "as happening so short
a time after the death of a life in being," Treby, C. J. "doubted
much of that and was of opinion that the time allowed for
executory devises to take effect, ought not to be longer than
the life of one person then in esse," and he cited *Snow* v. *Cutler*.
As the Court held that this particular devise was a contingent
remainder, no decision on the other point was necessary; but
clearly *Taylor* v. *Biddall* was not considered in either of these
cases as justifying a rule of lives in being and 21 years after.
The reason may be that though the form of devise "to A. for
life until B. reaches 21" might where B. was then unborn reach
the limit, yet when B. was born and A. was alive at his
majority, the devise would be within a life in being, i.e. A.'s,
and so the possible extension would not be suggested. And
certainly Lord North, who presided in *Taylor* v. *Biddall*, took
an entirely different view in the case of the *Duke of Norfolk*,
which we have for the moment passed over.

The Duke of Norfolk's case as the first reasoned discussion
of the rule is sometimes called *The Case of Perpetuities*[3]. The
deed in question was rather complicated, its object being to

---

[1] Showers, *Parl. Cases*, 137. Hargreaves, 36.

[2] 1 Ld. Raym. 203.

[3] 2 Chan. Rep. 119. Pollexfen, 223.
Lewis, *Perp.* 144. Hargreaves, 46.

secure the profits of certain lands to the second son of the Duke
of Norfolk, whoever he might be[1]. The lands were therefore
conveyed to the Duke for life, with remainder to trustees for a
term of 200 years, remainder to Henry the second son in tail,
remainder to Charles the third son in tail. Another deed
declared the trusts of the term of 200 years to be to pay the
profits to Henry, so long as Thomas the eldest son or his issue
male should survive, but if Thomas should die without issue
male, (in which case Henry would succeed as eldest son), then
the profits should be paid to Charles. Thomas died without
issue, and the question arose whether the trust of the term
claimed by Charles, limited after the trust to Henry and his
heirs male, was not too remote. The Chief Justices of the three
Common Law Courts advised the Chancery that it was void, but
the Chancellor, Lord Nottingham, upheld it as taking effect
within Henry's life, and therefore not leading to a perpetuity.
The judges had opposed, partly on the authority of some of the
older cases, and partly as leading to perpetuities, and Lord
Nottingham said : "as to the objection that was made 'where
shall it stop, for if it may be good after a limitation to a man
and his heirs determinable upon a contingency to happen in
the space of one life, so likewise for two lives, and so for twenty
lives.' To that he answered that Westminster Hall will quickly
stop it, when they find it tends towards a Perpetuity, or when
they find any inconvenience in it, but when the contingency is
to determine in one or two lives, there is none." In opposition
therefore to the view of his three Common Law Assessors, the
Chancellor affirmed the validity of the deeds : on his death his
decision was reversed on review, by Lord North, the then Lord
Keeper, but was reaffirmed on appeal to the House of Lords.

The effect of this decision, which proceeded on the ground
that terms of years were equally with estates of inheritance
subject to executory devises, was, according to Mr Hargreaves, to
create a general practice of settling terms of years, and providing
portions for children under the trusts of such terms, to the
extent of lives in being and 21 years after their expiration[2].

[1] The eldest son was a lunatic, hence   [2] p. 50.
the machinery.

For the *Duke of Norfolk's Case* was considered to support the principle "that so long as the strict settlement of any property, whether by executory devise or by similar trusts, did not exceed the ordinary time for barring a regular entail settled in estates for life with remainder in tail to an unborn child, which was when such child should attain 21, it was allowable." Although this practice followed with regard to terms of years, yet the case itself only gives authority for the creation of limitations to take effect within lives in being, in this following *Goring* v. *Bickerstaff*.

The extension of the term, during which freehold estates might be settled by executory devise, to 21 years after the expiration of lives in being was not formally recognized till the case of *Stephens* v. *Stephens* in 1736. Indeed in 1699 in the case of *Scattergood* v. *Edge*[1], Treby, C. J., in allowing as good a devise to the eldest son of A., (who had then no son), and his heirs male, and, if A. should die without issue then to the eldest son of B., (who had then issue), in tail, expressed very forcibly the strong dislike of the Common Law Judges to any extension of the limits of executory devises. "Since they have crept into the law", he said, "they have occasioned great confusion and disorder...they were utterly unknown to the common law, have obtained with much ado; and now they have prevailed, ought to be looked upon with much jealousy, lest they run to a perpetuity: and a perpetuity is such a condition of a fee that the feoffee shall not be able to give absolutely to another. It was a great policy of the Common law that alienations should be encouraged,...and these executory devises had not long been countenanced when the Judges repented them; and if it were to be done again, it would never prevail; and therefore there are bounds set to them, namely a life or lives in being and further they shall never go by my consent at law, let Chancery do as they please."

In *Stephens* v. *Stephens*, (1736)[2], there was a devise to a person unborn when he should attain the age of 21 years. The Chancellor referred the case to the Judges, who certified thus :

---

[1] 12 Mod. 278, 287.   [2] Cases temp. Talbot, p. 228.

"We do not find any case wherein an executory devise of a freehold hath been held good, which hath suspended the vesting of the estate until a son unborn should attain the age of 21 years, except the case of *Taylor* v. *Biddall*[1]. That resolution appeared on every view of it to be so considerable in the present case that we caused the record to be searched, and find it to agree in the material parts thereof with the printed report, and therefore, however unwilling we may be to extend executory devises beyond the rules generally laid down by our predecessors ; yet upon the authority of that judgment, and its conformity to several late determinations in cases of terms for years, and considering that the power of alienation will not be restrained longer than the law would restrain it ; viz. during the infancy of the first taker (in tail), which cannot reasonably be said to extend to a perpetuity ; and that this construction will make the testator's whole disposition take effect, which otherwise would be defeated ; we are of opinion that the devise before mentioned may be good by way of executory devise." To this certificate the Lord Chancellor, Lord Talbot, "was pleased to decree accordingly, and expressed his satisfaction with it, as agreeing perfectly with his own sentiments, and said he hoped it would be for the future a leading case in the determination of all questions of this kind."

In 1765, Blackstone states the law accordingly : " The utmost length that has hitherto been allowed for the contingency of an executory devise of either kind to happen in, is that of a life or lives in being, and 21 years after[2] " ; and in *Jee* v. *Audley*[3] in 1787, Sir Lloyd Kenyon, the Master of the Rolls, refers to the authority of the rule as to personalty thus : "the limitations of personal estate are void, unless they necessarily vest, if at all, within a life or lives in being, and 21 years and nine or ten months afterwards. This has been sanctioned by the opinion of judges of all times, from the time of the *Duke of Norfolk's Case* to the present : it is grown reverend by age, and is not now to be broken in upon."

A statute of 1699[4] had provided that children *en ventre sa*

---

[1] 2 Mod. 289; *supra*, pp. 125, 126.   [3] 1 Cox, *Cases in Equity*, 324, 325.
[2] Bl. II. 174.   [4] 10 and 11 Will. III. c. 16.

S.   9

mère at their father's death should, for all purposes of limitations of estates, be deemed to have been born in his lifetime; an enactment which necessarily converts the time of
" 21 years after lives in being," into " 21 years *plus* the time of
gestation." This rule was however treated by some judges as
merely an explanation of lives in being, the period of gestation
being treated as " an appendix of the life in being," and not a
new period. In *Long* v. *Blackhall*[1], (1797), this period of gestation was reckoned at the beginning of the period; that is to say,
an infant *en ventre sa mère* at the testator's death was reckoned
as a life in being, from whose death the 21 years would run; and
this would seem, though Mr Hargreaves disputes it, to allow
the period of gestation twice, once to make " the life in being,"
and once for the 21 years, or minority of a tenant after the
expiration of the life in being.

One more decision was necessary to give precision to the
rule. The period of "lives in being and 21 years after" was
probably derived by analogy from the practical effect of the
rule forbidding the limitation of remainders to the unborn child,
A., of an unborn child, B, in restraining alienation; but there
the 21 years was derived from the actual minority of B., at the
expiration of which he, as tenant-in-tail, could break the entail
and alien. The question arose whether in the case of executory
devises, the 21 years must relate to the actual minority of
some particular person or whether it was a term *in gross*, that
is to say, of 21 years from the death of the last "life in being"
irrespective of any minority or the condition of any particular
person. After an inconclusive discussion of the point in *Beard*
v. *Westcott*[2] in 1813, the question was clearly raised in 1827 in
the case of *Bengough* v. *Edridge*[3], afterwards decided by the
House of Lords under the name of *Cadell* v. *Palmer*[4]. There
land was devised to trustees for 120 years from the testator's
death, if 28 persons named in the will, or anyone of them,
should so long live, and for 20 years from the expiration or
sooner determination of the term of 120 years. This, it will be
seen, was in itself an ingenious machinery to secure that the

[1] 7 T. R. 100.
[2] 5 Taunt. 392.
[3] 1 Simons, 173—271.
[4] 1 Cl. and Fin. 372.

term "lives in being and 21 years after" should be as long as possible, by taking the survivor of 28 persons as the "life in being." Out of this term so created, a number of smaller estates were limited, some of which, as for instance an estate to — _ the son of an unborn person for 99 years if he should so long live, would, if standing by themselves and limited out of the fee, have been invalid. Here the term was treated as one *in gross*, and independent of the particular persons interested in the estate, and could only be sustained if such a view were valid. On this view both the Court below and the House of Lords in *Cadell* v. *Palmer* confirmed it. It was there held that a limitation by way of executory devise was valid, though not to take effect till after the determination of a life or lives in being, and within a term of 21 years from such determina- tion, as a term in gross, and without reference to the minority of any particular person. The time of gestation is only to be allowed where gestation actually exists.

This decision therefore finally establishes the definite limits of restraints on alienation, or the Rule against Perpetuities, in the case of executory devises. Though the rule seems to have been built up on the analogy of the rule relating to contingent remainders, it yet goes further than its model in two important respects. The rule as to remainders, which seems historically connected with Lord Coke's metaphysical objection to a possi- bility on a possibility, is that no estate can be limited after a life estate to a person unborn. The result was that the ordinary form of settlement became a series of life estates to persons in being, with a remainder in tail to a person unborn. If the tenant-in-tail were *en ventre sa mère* at the death of the last tenant for life, the land would be in effect restrained from alienation for a life or lives in being, and for 21 years plus the time of gestation afterwards, as it could not be dealt with till the tenant-in-tail attained his majority. But the tenant-in-tail might have attained his majority before the last tenant for life died, in which case the period of restraint would be 21 years shorter.

These restrictions differ in two important respects from those imposed on Executory Devises. I. In settlements by remainders the "lives in being" all take life estates in the land, and have a substantial interest in it: there is some reasonable connexion between the duration of their lives and the postponement of free alienation. But in Executory Devises, the lives in being may have no interest at all in the land; in the great case of *Cadell* v. *Palmer*, out of the 28 lives in being, 21 had no interest in the land at all, and it would be quite within the letter of the law to insert as the lives in being, all the boys at Eton on the testator's death, or all the members of the House of Lords at the same date.

II. While a settlement by remainders in tail depending on particular life estates can only last for 21 years after lives in being and may cease to restrain alienation at the death of the last tenant for life, according to the age of the particular tenant-in-tail, an executory devise, being founded on a term *in gross*, independent of the circumstances of any particular person, can always be contrived so as to restrict alienation for the full term of 21 years after lives in being; while these lives in being may, by arbitrary selection, be prolonged with all but certainty beyond the average duration of human life.

In the case of Executory Devises the rule against perpetuities is therefore much less strict and effective than is the corresponding rule with regard to remainders. This was recognized by the Real Property Commissioners, who recommended: (1) that lives in being by which to postpone the period of free alienation should not be arbitrarily taken, and that all lives should be deemed to be arbitrarily taken unless in the instrument creating the limitations each life appeared to be actually interested in the land. (2) That a contingent remainder or other future estate or interest which, if limited to take effect out of an estate in fee, would be void under the rule against perpetuities, should also be void if limited to take effect out of any estate less than fee simple; a suggestion designed to defeat the ingenious machinery in *Cadell* v. *Palmer* by which void limitations were rendered valid by the protection of a term of years.

An additional restriction was imposed on the power of a man to fetter his successors in dealing with the land, in consequence of the celebrated will of Mr Thellusson[1], who directed the income of his property to be accumulated during the lives of all his descendants living at his death, and on the death of the last of them to be divided amongst the heirs male of his three sons. It was calculated that this will might cause income to be accumulated for a hundred years, in which case the sum to be ultimately divided would be at least thirty millions. An Act was therefore passed in 1800[2], which provided that trusts for accumulation of income of land should only be valid during the life of the settlor, or for 21 years after his death, or during the minority of any person living or *en ventre sa mère* at the time of his death. This however does not affect dispositions of the land itself, which are still governed by the Rule against Perpetuities, but prevents testators from imposing still tighter fetters on the use of the land, by even restraining the expenditure of the income derived from it.

[1] *Thellusson* v. *Woodford*, 11 Ves. 112. Fearne, *C. R.* p. 538 note. Will.   *R. P.* 14th ed. p. 334.   [2] 39 and 40 Geo. III. c. 98.

CHAPTER X.

SUCH therefore being the restrictions which judicial legislation has imposed on the power of settling land so that it
shall not be alienable, we are now in a position to appreciate
the mixture of law and custom by which even this rule was
evaded, and land was, until the passing of Lord Cairns' Act,
practically fettered to a family in perpetuity.

In the early part of this century an ordinary settlement of
land, to take a very simple instance, was of this nature. On
the marriage of A., land was settled on him for life, with a
remainder in tail to his eldest son B. then unborn, and successive
remainders in tail to his other sons in order of seniority,
remainder to the heirs of A. in fee. B.'s contingent remainder
was protected by the device of trustees to protect contingent
remainders[1]. Unless A. had no sons at all, in which case he
had an estate in fee, A. had only a life interest in the land.
But if sons were born to him no alienation that he by himself
could make would defeat their interests, for he could only deal
with his own life estate in the land. B. also, unless he could
persuade his father to join with him in barring the entail, could
until he succeeded to the estate on his father's death, only
alienate his own interest in the land, that is an estate in the
land, so long as B.'s heirs survived, which was known as a *base
fee;* he could not affect A.'s life interest in the land nor bar the
estates tail in remainder of his younger brothers. Consequently

---

[1] This is a simpler form than exists in practice.

the land was safe from complete alienation by the tenant-in-tail alone, until he was in possession, and had attained the age of 21: but as soon as B., the tenant-in-tail in remainder, attained his majority, he was in a position to join with the tenant for life, A., in aliening or resettling the estate. On the coming of age of the eldest son therefore, and very frequently on the occasion of his marriage, a proposal was usually made to him that in return for a fixed annual allowance from his father he should join in a resettlement of the land, which would convert his estate tail into an estate for life, giving his eldest son unborn an estate tail in remainder, with successive estates tail to his other sons. This proposal, if assented to and carried into effect, had the result of postponing the time when the estate could be fully alienated for another generation, or from the time when B. the eldest son should come into possession of the land to the time when his eldest son should succeed. It was urged on the eldest son, a young man and necessarily inexperienced, by the prospect of an immediate and considerable increase in his income, which usually rendered his marriage possible, and by the strong traditions of the class to which he belonged, backed by the advice of his relatives and legal advisers. The disadvantages of his position have been summed up by Mr Cliffe Leslie in a passage that has become almost classical[1].

" It is commonly supposed that the son acts with his eyes open and with a special eye to the contingencies of the future and of family life. But what are the real facts of the case? Before the future owner of the land has come into possession, before he has any experience of his property, or of what is best to be done, or what he can do with regard to it, before the exigencies of the future or his own real position are known to him, before the character, number and wants of his children are learned, or the claims of parental affection and duty can make themselves felt, while still very much at the mercy of a predecessor desirous of posthumous greatness and power, he enters into an irrevocable disposition by which he parts

---

[1] *Fraser's Mag.* Feb. 1867. Cited Cobden Club *Essays*, p. 114.

with the rights of a proprietor over his future property for ever, and settles its devolution, burdened with charges, upon an unborn heir." Its advocates have represented it as "a solemn appeal from one generation to the next;" which is open to the answer that at least "the common interests of the nation should be represented in the more than diplomatic privacy of this negotiation between father and son. On closer examination this supposed solemn appeal to each generation dwindles to a hasty compact, dictated by somewhat sordid considerations of a momentary interest, to which the law lends the sanction of irrevocability."

Under this system the great estates of England became held by a series of life tenants each of whom had signalized his arrival at legal years of discretion by depriving himself of the power to deal freely with the land which must be his in the future, and by fixing the person to whom the land should devolve on his death before he had any knowledge of that person's character circumstances or ability, and indeed before he was even born.

The acts of the Reformed Parliament dispensed with the necessity of "trustees to bar contingent remainders", and established a personage known as the "protector to the settlement," usually the tenant for life in possession, whose consent by deed is now the only formality necessary to enable the tenant-in-tail in expectancy to bar the entail, not only against his heirs, but also against remaindermen and reversioners. But these changes had only the effect of simplifying the machinery of family settlements, and slightly cheapening their cost: they in no way interfered with the restrictions on alienation management and succession which family settlements imposed on the land. Indeed the opinion of the Real Property Commissioners, as expressed in their first Report, was that no changes were necessary in the system of family settlements[1].

"The owner of the land is, we think, vested with exactly the dominion and power of disposition over it required for the public good, and landed property in England is admirably made to answer all the purposes to which it is applicable. Settle-

---

[1] 1st Report, pp. 6, 7.

ments bestow upon the present possessor of an estate the benefit of ownership[1], and secure the property to his posterity. The existing rule respecting perpetuities has happily hit the medium between the strict entails of Scotch law, by which the property _ _ entailed is for ever abstracted from commerce, and the total prohibition of substitutions and the excessive restrictions of the power of devising established in some countries on the Continent. In England families are preserved and purchasers always find a supply of land in the market. A testamentary power is given which stimulates industry and encourages accumulation, and while capricious limitations are restrained, property is allowed to be moulded according to the circumstances and wants of every family[2]".

In 1856, however, greater power was given to the tenant for life, by an "Act to facilitate Leases and Sales of Settled Estates[3]," which, with the Acts amending it, was consolidated and improved by the Settled Estates Act of 1877[4]. The general tenor of these Acts was to allow greater power of leasing and sale to the tenant for life, subject in each case to the approval of the Court of Chancery. The Court might authorise leases and sales of settled estates and timber "if it should deem it proper and consistent with a due regard for the interest of all parties entitled under the settlement[5]". To this extent power was given to the tenant for life, after going through an expensive and complicated application to the Court, to deal with the land more freely than he could under the settlement; but even this had a limitation. The settlor's wishes were still to be sacred, for the powers contained in the Act were not to be exercised if an express declaration that they should not be exercised was contained in the settlement[6].

Another series of Acts gave power to tenants for life to obtain capital for necessary improvements from Public Com-

---

[1] Do they enable him to perform the *duties* of ownership?

[2] And often, it might be added, before the circumstances and wants of the family are known, or the family is born.

[3] 19 and 20 Vic. c. 120, amended by

21 and 22 Vic. c. 77, 27 and 28 Vic. c. 45, 37 and 38 Vic. c. 33, 39 and 40 Vic. c. 30.

[4] 40 and 41 Vic. c. 18.

[5] § 4.

[6] § 38.

missioners for drainage and other like purposes. But all these powers were so fenced round with safeguards and expensive formalities as to rather discourage than lead to their use, and a vast quantity of English land is still undrained.

In 1882 however, with the consent and concurrence of a Liberal Lord Chancellor, Lord Selborne, an Act introduced by a Conservative Lord Chancellor, Lord Cairns, was passed. The Settled Land Act[1], which usually bears the name of its author, goes in theory nearly as far in the direction of freeing the land, as it is possible to do while the system of family settlements and estates tail is maintained. Any serious step further must be in the direction of their abolition.

As the result of this Act, it is not going too far to say that all land in England and Wales held under any family settlement or similar disposition may now be sold or otherwise dealt with by the private person then entitled to its income as beneficial owner, in nearly every way in which a prudent owner would deal with it, except that the resultant purchase money cannot be treated as income, but must either be invested in specified securities, or capitalized in the land by making improvements or paying off incumbrances[2]. The scheme of the Act is to place the tenant for life in the position occupied by the Court under the previous Settled Estates Acts, and to make him the sole judge of the propriety of the particular improvements or dealings with the land contemplated, so long as they are within the classes of improvements and dealings sanctioned by the Act. Certain acts, such as the sale of the principal mansion on the settled estate, cannot be carried out without the intervention of trustees; certain others require an application to the Court. The honest attempt has however been made to reconcile the beneficial owner's power of freely dealing with the land with the settlor's power of determining the line in which the land shall descend. The settlor's power over his land has indeed been seriously curtailed, for the tenant for life can neither contract himself out of the Act, nor transfer his powers under the Act to any other person: neither can the settlor, by provisions in the settlement or otherwise, restrict the exercise by

---

[1] 45 and 46 Vic. c. 38.   [2] Wolstenholme's *Settled Land Act*, p. 7.

the tenant for life of the powers under the Act, though he may enlarge them. The settlor is still allowed to fix a line of succession for his land, or its money value, but he cannot tie his heirs to the land or place them under restrictions in the management of the land which he himself is no longer on earth to control.

The real criticism on this Act and on its forerunners may be suggested by a clause of the Act of 1877, which runs[1]: "Nothing in this Act shall be construed to create any obligation on any person to make or consent to any application to the Court, or exercise any power." In other words: "You may lead a horse to the water, but you can't make him drink." You may give a tenant for life power to improve or to sell, but you can't compel him to sell, or improve, if you do not provide him with a sufficient motive. Lord Cairns' Act provides the limited owner with the power, but the system of family settlements deprives him in most cases of any motive. He may not see any particular object in improving the land for the benefit of a successor whom he has not chosen, and with whom he may be at enmity. He may perceive no advantage in risking his own income for the benefit of others. A limited owner has but a limited interest in the land, and from a limited interest, only half-hearted dealings can be expected. The family evils alluded to in the next chapter are untouched by this Act, which still allows "the son to have the curse of his father, but the land (or money) of his grandfather.[2]" The true remedy, with great resulting advantages political, economical and domestic, is the entire abolition of all estates in land but those in fee simple.

Meanwhile further improvements can be made, even on the lines of Lord Cairns' Act. It only applies at present to private owners. It should be extended to corporations, especially to clergymen owning glebe lands: for a clergyman is especially unfitted to deal with land, and has not, as the tenant for life may have, even a personal interest in his successor, that he should make improvements for him. To such owners powers of sale may be fairly given. And it is questionable whether in the case of many corporate bodies, such as the Ecclesiastical Commissioners, this sale might not be made compulsory.

---

[1] § 53.   [2] Bacon's *Works*, vii. 635.

CHAPTER XI.

THE most important restrictions on the alienation of and succession to land at the present time are the Laws of Entail and Settlement, and the Law and Custom of Primogeniture.

Under the body of laws and customs which may be described as the Law of Entail and Settlement, it is possible for a landowner to settle the disposition and devolution of his land for a period which may extend to eighty or ninety years from his'death, subject only to the possibility of the sale, under Lord Cairns' Act, of the whole or part of the land, the purchase money being still held on the trusts of the settlement. To this there is annexed the custom of Re-settlement on the majority of the first tenant-in-tail, which postpones the time when free alienation, except under Lord Cairns' Act, will be possible, for an average period of thirty years.

The Law of Primogenitary Succession to land on intestacy is accompanied by and supports a custom of Primogenitary Devise. The policy of these restrictions and the arguments for and against any alterations in the law in the direction of more or less freedom of disposition of land, I now propose to consider.

The recent compilation and issue by Government authority of the record of English landowners, known as the "New Domesday Book[1]," has placed at our disposal greater accuracy of information as to the distribution of landed property in the United Kingdom. Previous to its issue, there was a

---

[1] Moved for by Lord Derby in the House of Lords, Feb. 19, 1872. Compiled, 1874, 1875.

statement common that, whereas at the time of the old Domesday Book the land of England was divided among more than 200,000 owners, in the nineteenth century, though far more land was in cultivation, it was held by only 30,000 landlords. This latter statement was based on the returns to the Census of 1861, in which only 30,766 persons described themselves as "landed proprietors"; but an examination of these entries showed that nearly half these "proprietors" were women, from which it was clear that many of the male landowners had returned themselves under other heads. The statement as to the old Domesday, based on the old Domesday figures which show roughly: 9000 tenants in chief and sub-tenants: 36,000 socmanni and liberi homines; 110,000 villani, 90,000 bordarii and cotarii; appears to me equally inaccurate. For it is now fairly clear that the *villani, bordarii* and *cotarii* were manorial tenants, holding, though often themselves freemen, by servile tenure, and not yet having attained such security of position that they can be reckoned as landowners in any modern sense of the word. And if this is so, the greater part of the land of England is owned immediately after the Conquest by the 9000 tenants in chief and sub-tenants, while the 36,000 *socmanni* and *liberi homines* represent the small proprietors, the sum of whose holdings would be insignificant beside those of the great lords. Mr Seebohm estimates the acreage of land in the manors at under 4 million acres, divided into 1½ million acres of the lord's demesne, 2¼ million acres held by *villani*, and a ¼ million held by *bordarii* and *cotarii*[1]. But from the landowner's point of view, these 4 million acres were held by the 7,800 sub-tenants, who in their turn were tenants of the 1400 tenants *in capite* who thus held 4 million acres of English land. The holdings of the 36,000 socmen Mr Seebohm estimates at 1 million acres. On these figures it is hardly fair to make any definite statement as to the distribution of the land without considerable explanation; but there are more substantial grounds for saying that it was held by 1400 landowners, than for dividing it amongst over 200,000.

---

[1] Seebohm, *V. C.* p. 102.

There can however be no question that shortly after the Black Death and throughout the 15th century, before the process of consolidation of farms and their enclosure for pasture land, induced by the entry of commerce into landowning, had destroyed many small holdings, English land was largely held by small proprietors. Fortescue in the reign of Henry VI. says, that in no country of Europe were small proprietors so numerous as in England. They were the yeomen of England, " freemen born in England, who may dispend of their own free land in yearly revenue the sum of forty shillings "..." These are they that in times past made all France afraid[1]."

The New Domesday, in spite of the great inaccuracies to be pointed out hereafter, at any rate provides materials for far more accurate generalisations as to the present distribution of land in England and Wales. It shows 972,836 proprietors of land, owning 33,013,510 acres, with a gross estimated rental of £99,352,303. These figures may be further dissected as follows:

Class of owners.	Number of owners.	Acreage of their lands.	Estimated rental.
Owning over 50,000 acres	4	376,554	£350,620
„ between 50,000 and 5,000 acres	870	8,990,474	12,190,935
„ „ 5,000 „ 1,000 „	4,534	9,328,497	17,439,682
„ „ 1,000 „ 100 „	37,116	10,145,024	20,108,311
„ „ 100 „ 10 „	98,479	3,541,684	10,811,291
„ „ 10 „ 1 „	121,983	478,679	6,438,324
„ under 1 acre	703,289	151,171	29,127,679

A table which by further division gives the result:

Owners of OVER 100 acres: 42,524 owning 28,840,549 acres, rental £50,089,548.

Owners of UNDER 100 acres; 923,751 owning 4,171,534 acres, rental £46,377,294.

And these tables show at first sight a considerable number of small owners, and a fair distribution of land. Closer investi-

---

[1] Harrison's *Description of England*, cited by Brodrick, p. 33.

gation however effects a great alteration in the aspect of the returns.

In the first place there are important omissions. The returns only refer to rateable land, and as, at the time they were made, woods wastes and commons were not rateable, some 4 million acres are excluded from the return, of which most of the wood and waste undoubtedly belongs to great landowners. Again, London is not included in the return. This omission excludes a number of large estates held by great landowners, such as the Dukes of Bedford, Portland, and Westminster, with an enormous rental and a still more enormous reversionary value.

Secondly, beside these omissions, the returns themselves contain fruitful sources of error. No attempt has been made to collect under one head the possessions of landowners in different counties. Thus the Duke of Buccleugh figures as 14 land-owners, the Dukes of Devonshire and Cleveland, Earl Howe and Lord Overstone as 11 each, and the Duke of Bedford as 10 : 6 great landlords thus appear as 68 lesser landowners[1]. And, as each peer is reckoned as a separate landowner in each county, some of his county holdings go to swell the ranks of small owners. Thus the Duke of Buccleugh counts as 9 owners of lands over 1000 acres, and 5 under 1000 acres, one of these holdings being a plot of eight acres, for which his Grace appears as an owner holding less than ten acres. Even in the same county the same lay owner appears through carelessness several times ; Captain Heathcote appears as 4 owners in Staffordshire ; an error which again tends to unduly swell the records of the small estates[2].

Another serious source of error occurs in dealing with the lands of corporations and of the church. The clergyman is frequently entered as the "owner" of glebe land, and as the glebes are usually of small acreage, the roll of small owners is proportionately enlarged. Thus in Buckinghamshire, there are only five parcels of glebe land returned, but 235 owners have the title "Reverend"; in Lancashire there are 286 clerical

[1] Arnold, *Free Land*, p. 5.
[2] See results of Mr Bateman's In-

vestigations. Brodrick, p. 189 *et al.*

owners but only seven pieces of glebe[1]. The same is the case
with corporations. "Churchwardens" appear in Norfolk as
136 owners: "charity" in Cambridge as 70 owners: "Trustees
of the Poor" account for 40 owners in Bucks, and the London
and North Western Railway figures as 28 owners in various
counties. All these errors tend to increase the apparent
number of small owners, while decreasing the roll of great
landlords.

Another fundamental source of wrong inferences suggests
itself on referring to the classified list of owners. Owners of
land under one acre hold roughly 150,000 acres with a rental of
£29,000,000, or nearly £200 per acre; owners of land over one
acre in extent hold their thirty-two million acres at a rental of
about sixty million pounds, or £2 per acre. While the 150,000
acres of the proprietors under one acre are rented at twenty-nine
millions, the 480,000 acres of the proprietors of from one to ten
acres are rented at £6,400,000; three times the land at less than
a fourth of the rental. Or to put it broadly, the four million acres
held in plots of under 100 acres are rented at 46 millions, whilst
the 29 million acres held in estates of over 100 acres are only
rented at 50 millions.

This striking difference points to a fundamental source of
error in the returns. Many of these small properties which
produce an average rent of £200 per acre must be residential
holdings on the borders of the towns. But these, even if owned
by their occupiers, can hardly be used to swell the number of
landowners in England, while it is more than probable that
many of these plots are in reality long leaseholds on ground
rents, and should therefore in fairness go to swell the records of
the great owners.

The importance of these numerous sources of error is shown
from the fact that Mr Bateman's analysis of the New Domesday
corrects the 5408 holders of land of over 1000 acres, with an
acreage of nearly 19 million, and a rental of 30 millions, to
4217 actual owners[2]. These necessary but difficult corrections
obviously render it impossible to formulate more than approxi-

---

[1] Arnold, p. 9.   [2] Brodrick, p. 165.

mate conclusions as to the distribution of land in England. Mr Brodrick estimates that 2250 persons own nearly half, or 4000 persons four-sevenths, of the land of England and Wales, and that there are 150,000 owners of land of over one acre in extent[1]. Mr Shaw Lefevre estimates the number of such owners at 165,000. Mr Arthur Arnold puts it under one hundred thousand, and places four-fifths of the land of the United Kingdom in the hands of 7000 persons[2]; Mr Kay, who does not allow for the errors of the New Domesday, estimates that 12,500 persons own two-thirds of the United Kingdom[3]. While, according to Mr Froude, the apologist of the present Land Laws: "the House of Lords does own more than a third of the whole area of Great Britain. Two-thirds of it really belong to great peers and commoners, whose estates are continually devouring the small estates adjoining them."

Detailed analysis of the returns shows conclusively that the land system of the United Kingdom, especially from an agricultural point of view, is one of large, often of very large, estates: and there can be no doubt that, up to the passing of Lord Cairns' Act, the effect of the system of settlements was to decrease the number, and increase the size, of properties in land. Land in settlement could not be sold, and adjoining land was constantly being added to it by ambitious proprietors, or trustees acting under trusts to purchase, for the purpose of increasing the family land; while no settlement ever contained provisions tending to decrease the size of individual holdings. Besides this increase in the size of landed estates there has been a corresponding consolidation of small farms, prompted by a desire to obtain economy in management and in expenses of farm buildings and to utilize new steam machinery more efficiently than can be done in the small fields.

This is hardly the place to fight over the old battle of Peasant Proprietorship against the system which makes the land support landlord, farmer and labourer. The evidence seems to me to point to the conclusions :—

(1) That for certain kinds of agriculture, such as market

[1] Brodrick, p. 166. [3] Kay, pp. 17, 18.
[2] Arnold, pp. 6, 11.

S. 10

vegetables, fruit, and the vine, small holdings, and *la petite
culture* are economically preferable to large ones.

(2) That for other kinds of agriculture such as corn, large
holdings are economically preferable. The same amount of
work and capital engaged in producing such crops will produce
more return on one large farm than on six small ones of the
same area.

(3) That from a social and national point of view, the
establishment of a class of peasant owners, hard working and
thrifty, touched by the "magic of property, which turns sand
into gold," working with the zeal of men who know that their
work is for their own benefit and their children's, is far more
desirable than the creation of a class of farmers holding by
custom on yearly tenancies without due security for their
improvements, or the maintenance of a class of labourers at
wages so low as to give little chance of saving, with no hope of
ever emerging from the bondage of a weekly wage, or escaping
the prospect of an old age in the poorhouse.

For the great national danger of the large estates of England
is that the small class of men who own the land of England are
forcibly brought into contrast and conflict with the great nation
who have to live on it.   Fortunately English landowners do not
avail themselves of their full legal rights, nor would the state
allow them to do so; else a few great landlords might depopulate
great tracts of country and lay London waste.   That the insistance by a landowner on the strict letter of the law is not
impossible is shown by the recent action of Mr Winans on the
vast Scotch moors he hires; while the dangers of such insistance
appear in the passions which his action has roused in the
neighbouring population of crofters.

Political stability is destroyed when the masses are landless,
and the landowners few; a sober and truly conservative
progress will be assured when the masses of the nation are
educated to the right use of political power, and have a stake
however small in the national land.   The present system of
large holdings is unsafe for the landlords and dangerous for the
country.

But besides this political and national evil of instability, there is the national and economical evil of large holdings starved of capital and imperfectly developed in resources. The tenant for life often succeeds to an estate heavily charged with portions to his mothers and sisters, rent-charges to his younger brothers, and interest on encumbrances created by past owners. He is expected to keep up a house, and position in the county, corresponding to his apparent and not to his real income. Under such circumstances how is it possible for him to make the necessary improvements in the property, or even to keep his farms in good order and his buildings in proper repair. Indeed, why should he ? The burden of the expenditure falls on him now; its benefit will generally be reaped by his successor, a successor whom he has deprived himself of the power of objecting to, and who will succeed to the land irrespective of his character, his ability, or the wishes of his predecessor. For years the land may be thus starved by limited owners, for as has been well said, "it is not conceivable that land will ever be handled by those who have only a closely restricted use of the land, or its purchase money, with anything approaching the freedom, promptitude or activity of those who can use the land or the money as they please[1]."

Thus in 1851, Mr James Caird reported that "much of the land of England...is in the possession of tenants for life so heavily burdened with settlement encumbrances that they have not the means of improving the land they are obliged to hold... one great barrier to improvement which the present state of agriculture must force on the attention of the Legislature is the great extent to which landed property is encumbered. In every county where we found an estate more than usually neglected, the reason assigned was the inability of the proprietor to make improvements on account of his encumbrances[2]." In 1878 the same eminent authority writes that the land held by tenants for life "is frequently burdened with payments to other members of the family and in many cases with debts.... There is no capital available for the improvements which a

---

[1] Lord Hobhouse, *Times*, Oct. 16, 1885. [2] *English Agriculture*: cited Arnold, 47.

landowner is called upon to make in order to keep his property abreast of the advances in agricultural practice[1]."

Mr Kay cites the case of a large estate of which he was trustee, which, on the marriage of the owner at 21, was settled on him for life with remainder in tail to his children. He plunged extravagantly into debt, sold his life interest to a Jew, and left England. "For forty years," says Mr Kay the trustee, "the farmers had no leases or security for any expenditure." Neither they, nor the Jew, nor the lessee of the mansion would spend any money on the land. "All social progress, and all social prosperity upon the estate were put an end to, the farm buildings fell into decay, the land was not properly drained or cultivated; the plantations were injured; the mansion became dilapidated[2]," and all through the settlements and restrictions allowed by the law. Lord Carrington's celebrated speech to his Buckinghamshire tenants in 1879, though inaccurate in some points, is to the same effect[3].

Much of the evidence before the Duke of Richmond's Commission on agriculture is to the same effect. Mr Charles Whitehead, the well-known agriculturist says: "In Kent there is a large estate comprising some of the finest land in the county, upon which no permanent improvements are being made, no buildings are being put up, nothing is done; the rent has been screwed up to the highest possible point...the present life tenant is at his wits' end to get money at all; he cannot live at the ancestral house; he lives in a comparatively small house and he certainly has not half enough to keep up his position as a nobleman....That estate has not been fully and properly developed, as it would be by a man who had it absolutely, and who could deal with it as he pleased[4]:" and he gives it as his opinion that "the improvements on the estate of an absolute owner certainly are more striking and marked than those upon the estate of an owner who has only a life interest." Mr Shaw Lefevre says[5]: "I think the system of entail has a

---

[1] *The Landed Interest and the Supply of Food*, cited Arnold, 48.
[2] Kay, p. 20.
[3] Cited Arnold, p. 15.

[4] *Minutes of Evidence*, 1881. C. 2778. qq. 56516; 56668.
[5] q. 64152.

very deleterious effect on the improvement of land. I have no doubt that a very large number of properties in this country are in the hands of persons who are so situated by reason of family entails and settlements that they are without the motive — — and without the means of improving their lands." Sir James Caird confirms his former testimony: he says[1] "I consider that the present system of the ownership of land is detrimental to the progress of English agriculture, because I think that the landowners who are under restraint in the management of their land cannot do full justice to it; and if the landowners of this country had full powers over the land unquestionably it would lead to a large development of its resources, which I think is at present much prevented....I am of opinion that landowners will find it necessary to have the utmost freedom of action in view of the great competition upon which we are entering with America. Entails are great evils." Mr Wolstenholme, the well-known conveyancer, and an upholder of the present system makes the significant remark: "Tenants for life effect improvements out of their income, wherever they are solvent owners[2]." But what of the tenants for life, who are not solvent? for in them one of the great evils of the system appears.

Lack of capital wherewith to make improvements decreases the productiveness of the land; proper drainage, the judicious opening of mines and quarries, liberal use of artificial manures, and suitable provision for preserving liquid manures, the construction of silos for the new and valuable device of ensilage, all are practically impossible to the burdened tenant for life, while where he has the power to borrow money, or to sell land, for the purpose of employing the resulting funds in making improvements, he will rarely have the interest or motive to lead him to do so, when much of the benefit will be reaped by a successor whom he has not chosen, and with whom he may be on terms of enmity.

Yet another national evil is to be found in the expense of the transfer of land: and this is rendered necessary by the complicated title by which under a will or a settlement land may be held. As Mr Shaw Lefevre says: "The possibility of carving

---

[1] qq. 62722, 62958, 62969.   [2] q. 55129.

out separate interests in land is the principal cause of the very great cost and complication of the transfer of land[1]." The movement to secure cheap land-transfer can only succeed by simplifying the title by which land can be held. The legal charges are or may be undoubtedly high, but they are high because the work to be done is intricate and difficult, and requires highly trained and highly paid skill. The more knots a man is allowed to tie in a piece of string, the more time and trouble it will take either to untie them all, or to see that they are all properly tied. "If you make all freeholds devolve exactly as leaseholds," says Mr Wolstenholme, a hostile witness and therefore of great weight, "I might burn three-fourths of the books on property law on my shelves : you would abolish everything connected with estates for life, contingent remainders and estates tail. There would be such a clearance made of the law that it would be most simple[2]." Again, no system of Registration of Title can be simple or cheap so long as titles of so complicated a nature have to be registered. And this expense of transfer from complexity of title, which at present must be incurred on each sale, and which is often as great on a small piece of land, as on thousands of acres, tells heavily on small purchasers, to whom the delay of investigation is onerous, and the great expense, still more its uncertainty, a fatal deterrent. The leisured man can wait for land; the rich man will think nothing of his solicitor's costs; but the land is already too largely held by these classes. Its dispersion among smaller holders would promote national stability and security ; and expense of transfer, or any cause which tends to prevent that dispersion, is on that ground alone objectionable.

Again, the system of large estates inevitably involves the existence of the absentee landlord, with the evils that absenteeism brings with it. The supervision of agents, however good, is a very inadequate substitute for the careful eye of a landlord whose land is his own.

The system of Family Settlements with its restrictions on alienation and its defined line of succession is therefore objectionable nationally and socially :

[1] q. 64168.   [2] q. 55153.

I. Because the owning of land by a small class produces a condition of unstable equilibrium in national life, instead of the security that results from the interest of the mass of the nation in the land.

II. Because the system of settlement deprives the limited owners it creates of both the power and the motive to effect the improvements in agriculture, necessary to secure to the land its greatest efficiency in producing power.

III. Because the system renders the transfer of land expensive, and thus hinders the lower classes from becoming small landowners.

But besides these national evils, serious disadvantages result to the family in whom and for whose benefit the land is settled. These evils Bacon's keen insight and prudent foresight described nearly 300 years ago in language so forcible that later writers have but followed in his footsteps. He is answering an imaginary objector who says[1]: "That it is a wisdom and foresight for every man to imagine of that which may happen to his posterity, and by all ways to establish his name. To that I answer that it is a wisdom, but a greater than even Solomon aspired after......For I find that he uses other language where he says that he must leave the fruit of his labour to one of whom he does not know if he shall be a wise man or a fool. And yet does he say that he shall be an usufructuary, or tenant restrained in a perpetuity? No, but the absolute lord of all that he had by his travail. So little did he know of these establishments......[2] Some young heir when he first comes into the float of his living outcompasseth himself in expenses, yet perhaps in good time reclaims himself, and has a desire to recover his estate; but has no readier way than to sell a parcel to free himself from the biting and consuming interest. But now he cannot redeem himself with his proper means, and though he be reclaimed in mind, yet can he not remedy his estate......Let us now consider the discipline of families......If the father has any patrimony and the son be disobedient, he may disinherit him; if he will not deserve his blessing, he shall

[1] *Chudleigh's Case.* Bacon, *Works.*   [2] p. 634.
Ed. Spedding VII. 632, *et seq.*

not have his living. But this device of perpetuities has taken
this power from the father likewise, and has tied and made
subject the parents to their cradle, and so, notwithstanding he
has the curse of his father, yet he shall have the land of his
grandfather."

Family settlements are injurious to parental control, for the
eldest son stands in a superior position to his father. His
succession is fixed beyond his father's control; his father's
interest in the land is less than his own. Should, as is too
frequently the case, family dissensions arise the father knows
that his expenditure on the land will be for the benefit of the
son with whom he has quarrelled; the son sees or imagines he
sees his father by act or by neglect injuring the land that must
come to him.

The land is settled on an unborn person without any regard
to his character or disposition; he may be a spendthrift, a
drunkard, a man devoid of all sense of his duty as a landlord,
but the land must come to him. His younger brothers may be
far more fitted to deal with the land than he; their father
might, if he had the power, choose them as the heirs of his land,
rather than his eldest son, the prodigal; but the deed of the
grandfather, who knew nothing of the future circumstances of
the family, but who bound the land so that it should come to a
particular child then unborn, be he the greatest scoundrel in
England, and the most unfit to manage a landed property,
prevails, to the injury of the land and its tenants, the family
and all its branches, and even of the eldest son himself, who has
frequently been strengthened in his evil courses by the sense
that do what he would the land must be his at the last.

Secure in this prospect, but poor till his father's death, he
anticipates his inheritance by encumbering the property, and
receives his land so burdened by the debts of his youth that all
hope of spending on it the capital necessary for its development,
or making savings with which to provide for his wife and
younger children without further encumbering the land, is gone.
And the family plunges deeper and deeper into debt, while still
the posthumous vanity of their ancestor, possibly approved by
their own family pride, ties them to the land they cannot or will

not either sell to free themselves from debt, or do justice to while they hold it.

The system of primogeniture in English family settlements has a further evil effect on the younger branches of the family. Dr Johnson's defence of primogeniture was that it secured there should only be one fool in the family, the eldest son who had no need to work for his living, as he saw before himself a safe future. But though the younger sons must in most cases earn their livelihood, the training they have received has not been such as to fit them for work. They have been brought up in the same mode of life as their elder brother the heir, have had the same, frequently useless, public school and university career and then find themselves left to face the world, almost entirely dependent on themselves for their own living, but unfitted by their training for earning it, while their elder brother, not by the fitness of things but by the accident of birth, inherits all the family land. The greatness of the family is secured by immolating its younger members on the family altar. This system has in past generations provided a crowd of claimants for public employment as of right, and the church and the public services have been flooded with younger sons, not for their competency, but because the system which produces cannot support them, but turns them on the country.

Then, until the passing of Lord Cairns' Act, the land was frequently burdened with restrictions as to its use, intended to protect the family interests against the individual, but resulting in the prevention of the proper development of the land. Long leases could not be granted, lest the heir should receive his land tied by the engagements of his predecessor; yet without long leases, great improvements could not be undertaken by the tenants. Capital could not be spent in experiments or doubtful ventures, however productive a successful result might be; mineral wealth could not be developed; drainage works could not be undertaken without complicated and expensive loans. The interests of the family in the land must be protected even though the interests of the family might suffer in the process; the risks that a good man of business would encounter for the profits that a good man of business would foresee must be sacrificed to the humdrum safety of cultivation on the old lines, however out of date.

The custom of primogeniture is so involved in the system of family settlements that many of the previous arguments apply equally against both, though the objections on the ground of injury to the family itself apply more especially to the custom which enriches one son and leaves his brothers in poverty.

The law of primogenitary succession in intestacy, which is the leading restriction on succession in the present day to which objection can be taken, stands on rather a different footing. By itself it has a tendency to encourage alienation, by transferring land to a single owner, without any restraint on his ownership. But its existence, so far as it tends to support the custom of primogeniture, is undesirable. The rule was introduced by feudal necessity, and perpetuated by legal ingenuity, rather than by historical and national policy. It is peculiar to England, and in England it has its only root in the feelings of the landed aristocracy. As has been well said, " the system is a very artificial one ; you may make a fine argument for it, but you cannot make a loud argument, an argument which would reach and rule the multitude. The thing looks like injustice[1]." If a great landowner dies without a will, it is thought natural that his lands should go by law to his eldest son, for such a succession is the custom of great landowners. But in many poor families with a little land, and among middle-class landowners who do not aim at founding a family, primogenitary succession is never thought of, and it is here when the landowner has neglected to make a will, or when his will is for some reason or other invalid, that great injustice is caused by the opposition of the line of succession provided by law to the private circumstances and probable wishes of the dead man. The cases are small and attract but slight attention, but the injustice is keenly felt in each family, and there are few solicitors who cannot supply instances from their own practice where the rule has worked to produce hardship. A solicitor at Birmingham, the owner of much small house-property, had

---

[1] Bagehot, *English Constitution*, Pref. p. xxxi.

made a will dividing it among his sons and daughters in equal shares; owing to changes in his family he desired to alter his will and gave instructions for that purpose to his younger son, the property being still to be equally divided. The son drew the will; it was duly signed and witnessed; and then, the father and younger son being alone in the father's study, the son said: "you had better destroy your old will." The father took the will out, tore it across, and put it back in his desk. On his death, the two wills were examined, but the new will, and not the old one, was torn across. The eldest son claimed all the land as in an intestacy, and the case was tried before a jury, there being only the evidence of the younger son, who was an interested witness, as to the circumstances under which the will was torn. Fortunately for the testator's intentions, the jury came to the conclusion that the second will was not torn *animo revocandi*, and it therefore stood; but if the son had not been with the father when the will was torn, and if the law of intestacy had operated, the father's wishes would certainly have been defeated, the State making a disposition of his land for him on his death which he himself would not have made in his life[1].

The different rules of succession for real and personal property appear the more indefensible, when the artificiality of the distinction between them is remembered. Railway and canal shares are usually personalty, while New River shares are realty; leases for 999 years are personalty, while leases for life are realty.

The existence of the law of primogeniture in intestate succession helps to support the custom of Primogeniture in testamentary succession and settlement. A striking illustration of this was seen when in the United States the law of Primogeniture was abolished, for a custom of equal division of land grew up, in spite of the powers of settlement possessed by American landowners.

Primogenitary succession in intestacy, which among small landowners is not the rule, and among great landowners works

---

[1] From private information.

mischief by helping to support a mischievous system should be abolished.

The arguments in favour of family settlements and primogeniture are difficult to state fairly, because as has been said, "being surviving peculiarities of feudal law, they can be defended only by those ingenious arguments which being manifestly begotten of after thought, appear convincing only to persons who need no conviction."

It is said in the first place that "a man has a right to do what he likes with his own," or in the form of the Duke of Richmond's continual question to witnesses before the Royal Commission, "Would it not be very tyrannical to prevent a father and son making what arrangement they please as to the land?" But this right is subject to the legal rights of others and to the condition that the use a man makes of his property shall not be prejudicial to the State. Nothing is more common than State interference with land, either in taking it for the purposes of the State, or in preventing it from being so used as to injure either the State or individual citizens. "A man's right to do what he likes with his own" is continually limited in this way by the State during his life; much more so after his death. He cannot take his property out of this world, but it has been considered conducive to industry and in accord with public policy to allow him to prescribe to whom his land should pass on his death; whether he should be allowed to impose restrictions, which the State would enforce, on the use of the land after his death, must depend on whether such restrictions are on the whole for the benefit of the community. The State has constantly interfered with dispositions of land at death; by the Statutes of Mortmain, it has prohibited their being made for ecclesiastical purposes; in the case of charitable devises, it has stepped in to change the dispositions which the testator had made; and in the very case of Settlement of land, it has already in the Rules against Perpetuities declined to sanction restrictions on the land which extend beyond a certain period. Any question of further restrictions on the power of disposition over landed property must be a question of degree of public convenience, and not of right, and as a question of public convenience the problem has been treated by Lord Nottingham and other judges who have specially allowed extensions of this power of disposition.

On the other hand while there is no *right* in a landowner to call upon the State to enforce all the directions which he may give for the use and management of the land which once was his, extending for forty, sixty or a hundred years after his death, neither is there any *right* in his children to claim all or any portion of his land unless in cases where their father has raised expectations of a particular mode of division, on which their habits and lives have been shaped.

It is alleged in favour of the system of primogenitary settlement that it is useful in maintaining a hereditary peerage. This assumes that an hereditary peerage should be maintained, a point which in 1885 can hardly be considered one of universal agreement. And if a hereditary peer is the better for the possession of sufficient property to ensure independence, this can be secured by the free power of devise in fee simple, which can be exercised by an hereditary peer in the interests of his order and his family.

But it is said that the preservation of ancient families can only be effected by some such means as this. It may be answered that families worth preserving will preserve themselves; that protection of ancient families is only needed against those of their members who are spendthrifts and scapegraces. For honourable and intelligent men may be trusted to do their duty to their family and the land without restrictions from without; it is the worthless members of families who must be bound. But this means that men unfit to be landowners must yet be tied to their land, and the land and its tenants will suffer accordingly. They would be benefited by transfer to another lord, but they are tied to a careless and improvident landlord, who cannot free himself if he would, for the sake of his family. To preserve worthless but ancient families is hardly a sufficient justification for checking the development of English lands, and hampering the agriculture of English tenants.

The general social effects of primogeniture and settlement are also enlarged on; it is said to create a leisure class, a resident proprietary, whose co-operation in county government is invaluable, and whose despotic but kindly rule showers blessings on their parish and district. But with large estates, large portions of them must inevitably lose the blessing of a resident landlord; and though the rule of the ideal great landowner may be beneficial, the rule of the actual one, tested by experience, has hardly proved so in all cases. The squires and their allies, the clergy, have had undisputed sway over rural England for centuries; what account can they give of their stewardship with regard to the labourer who has worked on their land? How can they justify the cottages they have provided for him; how can they defend as sufficient the provisions they had made for his education before the passing of Mr Forster's Act; how can they regard the position which the agricultural labourer is taking at the present time[1] as any other than a just recompense for centuries of neglect by those who have had the power to help them. While some settled estates have been admirably managed, too many of such estates, held by encumbered life tenants who cannot afford to live in their own mansion, bear eloquent testimony to the evils of limited ownership under the English land-system.

The system of entails and settlements is therefore to be condemned both in the interests of the nation, whose development it obstructs, and in the interests of the families it is intended to preserve. It injures the nation by producing political instability, by depressing the classes of farmers and labourers, and by hindering the adequate cultivation of the land. It is hurtful to the families by placing land in improper hands, by destroying proper parental control, by rearing up younger children in a manner which unfits them for their work in the world, and by hindering the proper development of the land in the interests of the family. On all these grounds it is desirable that all powers of settlement, or devise of land, other than a simple grant or devise in fee simple should be swept away, so that every landowner should be the absolute and unrestricted owner of his land[2].

---

[1] Written November, 1885.

[2] Whether an exception should be made in favour of life estates to widows is perhaps arguable, though I think the proposal in the text is preferable.

CONCLUSION.

I have now completed the task I proposed to myself at the _ _ outset. I have endeavoured to trace step by step and in historical sequence the growth and change of the Land Laws of England, and the motives of policy which prompted the legislation of the Parliament, the construction of the judges, and the evasive devices of landowners and their legal advisers. The pride of the owners of land has fettered their families to their estates: " *Te teneam moriens* is the dying lord's apostrophe to his manor, for which he is forging those fetters that seem by restricting the dominion of others to extend his own." The intricacies of the family settlement, while they add to the costs of transfer of land, hinder its development in the hands of a limited owner, and weaken the nation whose masses they leave landless and at the mercy of a small but wealthy class. All things point to the conclusion already expressed in this essay, and set out more than 200 years ago by an anonymous pamphleteer : "It were convenient that there might be no estate but absolute, for life or inheritance, without condition or entails, whether given by will or purchased by deed in writing; and this would shorten all suits about estates[1]."

[1] 3 Jurid. Soc. 598, from pamphlet of 1648.

INDEX.

S. 11

CAMBRIDGE: PRINTED BY C. J. CLAY, M.A. & SONS, AT THE UNIVERSITY PRESS.